Tantric Kali

"*Tantric Kali* provides depth as we are guided through mythology, ritual, visualization, and life teachings to have a direct experience of Shakti from the wisdom teachings of the Kaula path. Daniel offers another treasure from the heart of his realization—steeped in his lineage with translations of the oldest ritual to Kali—songs and hymns and truly transformative practices and meditations direct from the root. A full-spectrum offering, this is the birth of another Odier classic. Daniel is one of the extraordinary and skillful practitioner-teacher-scholar-writers of our time. *Tantric Kali* is juicy, liberating, radical, and exquisite and offers a unique compendium of tantric Kali sadhana accessible to all."

SHIVA REA, YOGINI,
FOUNDER OF SAMUDRA GLOBAL SCHOOL FOR
LIVING YOGA, AND AUTHOR OF
TENDING THE HEART FIRE

Praise For The Author's Previous Book
Tantric Quest

"Daniel Odier's story is the stuff of dreams for the spiritual seeker. Until this book, we have had few (if any) modern first-person accounts of a Westerner's initiation into tantrism. *Tantric Quest* fulfills our longing to understand this mysterious method and does so admirably, describing a path where sensual delight is married with full attention to re-create our birthright of life in the garden of the Goddess."

YOGA JOURNAL

Tantric Kali

Secret Practices and Rituals

DANIEL ODIER

Translated by Jack Cain

Inner Traditions

Rochester, Vermont • Toronto, Canada

Inner Traditions
One Park Street
Rochester, Vermont 05767
www.InnerTraditions.com

SUSTAINABLE FORESTRY INITIATIVE — Certified Sourcing
www.sfiprogram.org
SFI-00854

Text stock is SFI certified

English Language Edition arranged through Montse Cortazar Literary Agency (www.montsecortazar.com).

Library of Congress Cataloging-in-Publication Data

Names: Odier, Daniel, 1945- author.
Title: Tantric Kali : secret practices and rituals / Daniel Odier ; translated by Jack Cain.
Other titles: Kali. English
Description: Rochester, Vermont : Inner Traditions, 2016. | Includes bibliographical references and index.
Identifiers: LCCN 2016018632 (print) | LCCN 2016042151 (e-book) | ISBN 9781620555590 (paperback) | ISBN 9781620555606 (e-book)
Subjects: LCSH: Kālī (Hindu deity)—Cult. | Kashmir Śaivism. | BISAC: BODY, MIND & SPIRIT / Spirituality / Divine Mother, The Goddess, Quan Yin. | RELIGION / Hinduism / Rituals & Practice.
Classification: LCC BL1225.K32 O3513 2016 (print) | LCC BL1225.K32 (e-book) | DDC 294.5/2114—dc23
LC record available at https://lccn.loc.gov/2016018632

Printed and bound in the United States by Lake Book Manufacturing, Inc. The text stock is SFI certified. The Sustainable Forestry Initiative® program promotes sustainable forest management.

10   9   8   7   6   5   4   3   2   1

Text design by Priscilla Baker and layout by Debbie Glogover
This book was typeset in Garamond Premier Pro with AlParmaPetit, Optima LT Std, and Futura Std as display fonts

To send correspondence to the author of this book, mail a first-class letter to the author c/o Inner Traditions • Bear & Company, One Park Street, Rochester, VT 05767, and we will forward the communication, or contact the author directly at **www.danielodier.com.**

Contents

Preface

A certain number of practices that I received directly from my teacher Lalita Devi are not part of any treatises that I am aware of. I received my knowledge of the rituals and secret practices from her. Concerning the rituals of Kali, I also benefited from the magnificent presence of Shri Maa, a yogini disciple of Ramakrishna, who lives in the Napa Valley in California and who is a great admirer of Kali.[1] I never practice the ritual without donning the *rudraksha* (seed of Shiva) necklace that she gave me.

KRIM: the seed syllable (bija mantra)
of Kali

Kali and
the Tantric Path

*T*he mention of Kali evokes a shadowy world cloaked in mystery, for this Indian goddess emerged from humanity's ancient past. Although she has been worshipped for centuries, most of the treasures of her mythology and practices still remain virtually hidden in Sanskrit texts and esoteric sects. But Kali has many gifts for us.

"I am Great Nature, consciousness, happiness, the quintessential," says Kali in the *Chudamani Tantra*. She is the Cosmic Mother, dark as storm clouds, naked with wild hair falling to her knees. She comes to us from a rich past devoted to the worship of feminine power—a veneration of the Great Mother that was universal before the advent of religions. The civilization of the Indus Valley is where we find the seeds of the great ideas that were to form the movement that revered the Great Goddess. Terra-cotta statues of her can still be found, dating back 4,500 or 5,000 years. Paleolithic sites represent the Goddess in the form of triangular stelae or rounded rocks, some of which are still worshipped in India.

Kali sprang forth from pre-Vedic (before 1500 BCE) rural traditions that were wild and shamanic before migrating slowly into Indian tradition. She was perhaps the ancient goddess worshipped by the inhabitants of the Vindhya mountain range, which separates north from south in the center of India.

According to Sir John Woodroffe (Arthur Avalon), writing in the *Garland of Letters,* "Kali is the deity in that aspect in which It withdraws all things which it had created into Itself. Kali is so called because She devours Kala (Time) and then resumes Her own dark formlessness."[1] He quotes the *Mahanirvana Tantra* as follows:

> At the dissolution of things it is Kala (Time) who will devour all and by reason of this He is called Mahakala and since Thou devourest Mahakala Himself It is Thou who art called the Supreme Primordial Kalika. . . . Resuming after Dissolution Thine own nature dark and formless, Thou alone remainest as One, Ineffable, and Inconceivable.[2]

Kali speaks to us of the darker aspects of nature and our own human nature, yet she also speaks to us of love, for she became the consort of Shiva, adopted by tantric* practitioners

---

Tantric is the adjective form of *tantra,* which literally means "loom, warp," hence "principle, continuum, system, doctrine, theory," from the verbal root *tan,* "stretch, extend, expand," and the suffix *tra,* "instrument."[3] The *Kamika Tantra* gives the following explanation of the term *tantra:* "Because it elaborates (*tan*) copious and profound matters, especially relating to the principles of reality (*tattvas*) and sacred mantras, and because it provides liberation (*tra*), it is called a *tantra.*"[4] *Tantra* thus refers to both texts and to a tradition of beliefs and practices.

of the Kaula path. Kaula is the *vamachara* path, often called "the left-hand path," but because *vama* also means "woman," it would be more accurate and in harmony with the Kaula path to translate *vamachara* as "the Shakti path."

In the realm of Tantra, "the central theme is the divine energy and creative power (Shakti) that is represented by the feminine aspect of any of various gods; personified as a *devi*, or goddess, she is portrayed as his wife, above all as the wife of Shiva."[5] The tantric texts usually take the form of a dialogue between Shiva and Shakti. Kali, or Kalika, is one of the many forms of Shakti, whose name and form parallel that of the particular aspect the god takes, such as Kala and Kali, Bhairava and Bhairavi.[*]

The world of Kali is huge. It would be presumptuous to think that I could treat the whole of it, but I did want to bring together in one book the essentials of the mythology, rituals, and practices as well as the mystical worldview that they represent. Here you will find several texts that are being published in English for the first time.

Chapter 1 explores Kali's origins and symbolism, which will make it clear from the outset that she will be our guide to territory of the human psychophysical being that is usually scorned or forbidden in religion.

In chapter 2 the Kaula path and its spread across India is described in greater detail, with glimpses into the fecund field of Kali mythology, as well as an introduction to the thirty-six principles of reality (*tattvas*). This chapter includes

---

[*]In Indian mythology each god or goddess takes many forms and is known by many names. Each particular manifestation, such as Kali, can also have numerous particular names, each representing a specific aspect of that deity.

translations of the *Kaula Upanishad* and the *Kularnava Tantra,* which makes it clear that the value system of the Kaula tradition is very nonconformist.

Kali, however, is still able to speak to us, primarily through practices we enliven within our own beings. Chapter 3 introduces preliminary practices that are essential preparations for entering into Kali's profound rituals of transformation.

Chapter 4 contains the first publication of an English translation of the *Nirrutara Tantra,* the oldest presentation of the Kali ritual.

The Kali ritual is presented in detail in chapter 5, culminating in the ritual of Sacred Union.

Practices and visualizations to guide the aspirant along the Kaula path are given in chapter 6, including a focus on the eight chakras and sixty-four yoginis, the Yogini's Practice of the Heart, and the Devouring of Inner Demons.

In addition to inspiring the composition of many tantric scriptures, Kali has also evoked devotion in the form of hymns and songs, several of which are presented in chapter 7.

Civilization has brought us many marvelous things, but it has also cut us off from our ancient roots and from our connection to nature, to animals, and to the cosmos. The arrival of religions has added all sorts of regulations and rules, which have repressed our fundamental connections with the world. We have become frightened, conformist, moralizing, guilty, and terrified by these impulses that violently surge up in us, sometimes in sexuality and sometimes in confrontations. They can astonish us and shock us.

This is the context in which the practices of Kali are invaluable for today's practitioner. They allow us to reintegrate all of the volcanic impulses that flow through us in the labyrinths of imagination and dreams. As a presence that was established before the great religious movements, Kali has the power to reconnect us to our roots, to restore the complete range of what it means to be human, to offer us acceptance of all our richness—she encompasses the whole history of humanity from the first babblings to its final development.

Kali's Origins and Symbolism

THE BIRTH OF KALI

According to the mythology, Kali sprang forth from the third eye of the Great Goddess Durga, who was unable to overcome the demons, led by Canda and Munda, sent to oppose her in a cosmic war. She concentrated her powers in order to produce an incarnation of absolute violence and lanced Kali onto the battlefield. The story is related in the *Devi-Mahatmya,* written about twenty-five hundred years ago.

> 7.2 Then they saw the Goddess, smiling slightly, mounted
>   on her lion on the great golden peak of the highest
>   mountain. [3]
> 7.3 Having seen her, they made ready in their efforts to
>   abduct her,
>   While others approached her with swords drawn and
>   bows bent. [4]

7.4 Ambika* then uttered a great wrathful cry against them,
And her face became black as ink in anger. [5]

7.5 From the knitted brows of her forehead's surface
immediately
Came forth Kali, with her dreadful face, carrying sword
and noose. [6]

7.6 She carried a strange skull-topped staff, and wore a
garland of human heads;
She was shrouded in a tiger skin, and looked utterly
gruesome with her emaciated skin. [7]

7.7 Her widely gaping mouth, terrifying with its lolling tongue,
With sunken, reddened eyes and a mouth that filled the
directions with roars. [8]

7.8 She fell upon the great Asuras† in that army, slaying
them immediately.
She then devoured the forces of the enemies of the gods. [9]

7.9 Attacking both the front and rear guard, having seized
the elephants
Together with their riders and bells, she hurled them
into her mouth with a single hand. [10]

7.10 Likewise having flung the cavalry with its horses and the
chariots with their charioteers
Into her mouth, she brutally pulverized them with her
teeth. [11]

7.11 She seized one by the hair, and another by the throat.
Having attacked one with her foot, she crushed another
against her breast. [12]

---

*Ambika is another name for the Great Goddess.
†Demons.

7.12 The weapons and missiles that were hurled by the demons
     She seized with her mouth, and crunched them to bits
     with her teeth. [13]

7.13 The army of all those mighty and distinguished demons
     She destroyed: she devoured some, and thrashed the
     others. [14]

7.14 Some were sliced by her sword, others pounded with her
     skull-topped staff.
     Just in this way did the Asuras meet their destruction,
     ground up by the edges of her fangs. [15]

7.15 Immediately upon seeing the entire army of the Asuras
     slain,
     Canda rushed at the incredibly fearsome Kali. [16]

7.16 The great Asura enveloped the dread-eyed female with a
     horrendous great shower of arrows,
     And Munda did the same with discuses hurled by the
     thousands. [17]

7.17 This stream of discuses entering her mouth
     Resembled a multitude of suns entering into the middle
     of a black cloud. [18]

7.18 Then Kali, her ugly teeth gleaming within her dreadful
     mouth,
     Angrily cackled with terrible sounds. [19]

7.19 Mounting her great lion, the Goddess ran at Canda,
     And having seized him by the hair, she cut off his head
     with her sword. [20]

7.20 On seeing Canda slain, Munda rushed at her.
     She caused him to fall to the ground, wrathfully
     smitten with her sword. [21]

7.21 On seeing Canda slain, and also the valorous Munda,

What was left of the assaulted army was overcome with
fear and fled in all directions. [22]

7.22 Picking up the heads of Canda and Munda, Kali
Approached Candika* and spoke words mixed with
loud and cruel laughter: [23]

7.23 "Here, as a present from me to you, are Canda and
Munda, two beasts slain in the sacrifice of battle. Now
yourself can slay Sumbha and Nisumbha."[1]

Kali destroyed the demons, but she was so intoxicated by
her own power that she could not stop and began to kill the
gods. Durga then appealed for help from Shiva, who lay down
among the dying bodies. His beautiful eyes and his erect
lingam (phallus) calmed Kali, who allowed herself to slip
onto him and discover her capacity to incarnate absolute love.
The surprise of penetration was such that her tongue leaped
outward from her lips to point down to her heart. Thereafter
Kali was venerated by tantric practitioners as the incarnation
of power and of absolute love.

THE SYMBOLISM OF THE BODY AND
ATTRIBUTES OF KALI

Kali is black or midnight blue. All colors blend together in
the dark. Kali unifies duality; all manifestation disappears
in the black. "Just as all colors disappear in black, all names
and all forms disappear in her," says the *Mahanirvana Tantra.* Kali is the final fusion of appearances in the reality of

---

*Candika is another name for the Great Goddess.

the Self. She transcends all form. She is worshipped during the black moon, around funeral pyres, and during cremation chants. She is worshipped Tuesdays at midnight. She loves deserted places and crossroads.

Her worshippers, however, see her as luminous. Ramakrishna points out that "you see Her as black because you are far away from Her. Go near and you will find her devoid of all colour. The water of a lake appears black from a distance. Go near and take the water in your hand, and you will see that it has no colour at all. Similarly the sky looks blue from a distance. But look at the atmosphere near you; it has no colour."[2]

"I am Great Nature, consciousness, happiness, the quintessential," says Kali in the *Chudamani Tantra*. She is the Cosmic Mother, dark as storm clouds, naked with wild hair falling to her knees. Kali creates the cosmos, the elements, and language through the fifty severed heads of her necklace. She is sometimes represented as a dazzling adolescent, and sometimes in her terrifying and gaunt aspect. A crescent moon shines on her forehead; precious stones brighten her body. Her *yoni* (female sexual organ; womb, origin, source) is open to the world. Her tongue sticks out from a bloody mouth. Patches of blood are splashed on her body. Each aspect of her appearance in her various forms has potent meaning, which educates and enlightens her devotees.

Nudity: Kali is dressed in space; she is space. Her nudity symbolizes the fact that she is free of illusion's finery. She is nature. She is without name and without form. In enlightened consciousness, she is ultimate truth.

Three eyes: Kali's three eyes represent the sun, the moon, and fire, as well as the three times—past, present, and future— which she abolishes with her absolute presence. She is the destroyer of time.

Her breasts: In many paintings Kali's breasts are decorated with diagrams, which represent the cosmos linked to her heart center. They are covered in blood, in red, the color of Kali's passionate bursting forth. Her breasts are also a symbol of the generous mother. Kali's worshippers call her "Ma"—the Mother.

In a story from mythology (in a different version than the one related above), when Shiva is called upon by Durga to help appease Kali, he does not use the power of his lingam. Instead, he transforms himself into an infant in order to bring out Kali's protective and maternal instinct. This is how her worshippers see her: they become infant Shivas who suckle life, audacity, and nonconformism at the breasts of the Goddess.

Her open yoni: Her yoni contemplates the cosmos. In certain visualizations her clitoris becomes the eye that contemplates the infinite, bringing heaven and earth together. It is from the yoni that the lingam emerges, meaning that the strength of Shiva, the architect of the world, emerges from the absolute power of the feminine. The power of Shakti is symbolized by the final "i" of her name, which she transfers into the name of Shiva to give him the power. Without this "i" Shiva would be Shva, which in Sanskrit means a body stripped of its strength. Without Shakti, Shiva would be inert.

In the third chapter of the *Yoni Tantra* the eight goddesses, or powers, of Shakti are placed on the yoni, which is worshipped as the dwelling place of the goddesses. Its essence is absorbed by the yogi. Kali and Tara are in the chakra of the yoni. Chinamasta is the pubic fleece. Baglamukhi and Matangi are the labia majora. Mahalakshmi, Shodasi, and Bhuvaneshvari are hidden inside the yoni. "The insertion of the lingam into the yoni is a great *sadhana* [spiritual practice]. The most important thing in the recitation of the mantras and the sadhana is the flow of sperm and of pleasure."[3] The yoni is considered to be the essence of the cosmos. "What interest is there in bathing in the Ganges and visiting the sacred sites? Nothing equals devotion to the yoni. . . . The sadhana of the yoni is the greatest sadhana."[4] In several Tantras it is asserted that absorption of the sublime essence of the yoni cures illnesses. "Women are divine, women are life, women are real jewels."[5] The *Yoni Tantra* makes a close connection between the sadhana of Kali and the adoration of the yoni. This liberates the yogi from all energies of the *pashu*—the crude man—and transforms him into *vira,* or hero.

Kali's four arms: Kali's arms represent the cycle of creation and destruction, the cosmic rhythm, the circular nature of life and death in continual movement. When she is not carrying the trident, Kali's hand adopts the mudra that extinguishes fear and gives the courage to confront the real.

Menstrual blood: In the Kaula tradition, woman is the Goddess and menstrual blood is the manifestation of her power. Kali's blood (some paintings depict it flowing out of the yoni) is considered to be a divine nectar. It is used in rituals, sometimes mixed with sperm and wine. There is no taboo about a woman's period. On the contrary, it is venerated: the yoginis, preferably during their periods, couple with the yogis to transmit their power to them. When the yogi ejaculates, he kneels before the Shakti and absorbs the sun (blood) and the moon (sperm) in order to integrate the cosmos.

The cleaver or the sword: Kali cuts away inner mental dialogue. She allows the body to join the whole without allowing mental activity to introduce duality into the experience. The sword opens to silence; the silence opens to joy.

The trident: The trident symbolizes that the practitioner is at one and the same time the Divine, the temple, and the worshipper—all three brought together in a single branch.

The severed head: The severed head symbolizes mental silence and being rooted in the Self.

The cup: This vessel receives and holds the flow of mental associations that duality creates.

The skirt of severed arms: Severed arms represent the connection to action and therefore to karma, which, in its immediacy, is considered connected to the cosmos. All action is dependent on the totality of cosmic movement. There is no long-term predetermination; instead, just immediate connection in which everything enters into communication, pushing each being to actions that cannot result from a choice since everything is conditioned by the cosmic rhythm. The perception of the absence of choice leads to freedom, and the yogi exercises this freedom outside all frameworks or limits. He becomes *sahajya,* a spontaneous being, and acts from his own good will. In an absolute sense there is neither good nor bad—everything comes into balance in the infinite. No merit or demerit. No mistake, no glorious act. All that remains is the cosmic game in which we are only particles—free, dancing electrons.

The severed arms also mean that Kali slices off the arms of men who act in the world without awareness and especially women who are unaware of their bodies.

Her wild hair: Kali's hair represents revolt against social norms and freedom. It also represents the yogi's hair, which taps in to cosmic energy.

The jackals: While Durga rides a lion—the ultimate noble animal—Kali is the companion of jackals whose dark silhouettes blend into the night, often illuminated by the flickering light of funeral pyres. This symbolizes Kali's taste for forgotten or despised creatures. She also likes crows. Kali has the same attitude socially: she welcomes to her ceremonies all worshippers regardless of caste, history, or culture. She makes no such distinctions. The brahmin and the pariah are welcomed in the same way by the Mother. She administers her love to all. Her fearsome aspect is there only to push her devotees to gain the courage needed to go beyond the limitations of the mind, beyond the limitations of the beautiful and the ugly, the pure and the impure, the worthy and the unworthy.

The serpents: The serpents too are objects of fear and rejection. Kali, just like Shiva and all ascetics, lives in perfect harmony with serpents, whether they are poisonous or not. Often a king cobra protects Shiva. In the north of India, I have seen serpents playing with an ascetic's trident (symbol of Shiva) stuck in the ground, wrapping themselves around its tines. The serpent is also the link between heaven and earth, between the first and the last *tattvas* (principles of reality). The undulating movement of its body reminds us of the absence of dogma, beliefs, certitudes—an absence that bestows on the yogi the subtlety, grace, and power to detach from the limitations of the body, just as the serpent sheds its old skin.

The serpent also symbolizes eternity. In the dance of *tandava* (see page 16) the spinal column is thought of as a serpent. The head of the serpent is represented by the sacrum, and its tail ends at the occiput. The serpent is also the representation of Kundalini, which is not just an energy—it is also the Goddess coiled up in the heart rather than in the root chakra. This reflects the Kashmiri approach in which everything is centered in the heart. It is not the theme of a practice, but rather it is a grace: "This most high and subtle energy is seen to transcend all practices. When this energy encloses within itself the *bindu* [metaphysical point] of the heart, it is coiled like a serpent in deep, deep sleep. And there, in the heart, it remains in sleep, thinking of nothing. O Uma, this Goddess also has enclosed in her breast the moon, fire, the sun, the stars and the fourteen worlds but she is unconscious, as if a poison has drugged her."[6]

The cremation field: This field is where the five elements, the ego, and differentiation are destroyed and where the many are returned to the one, to ashes, to the earth, to the sky, to space. It is the end of concept, truth, and dogma. The end of emotional limitation. Here the five *kancukas** dissolve.

Tandava: Tandava is the dance of creation and of dissolution. It is the dance in which Shakti will vanquish Shiva, reestablishing the power of the feminine, imposing her rhythm and inviting us in our turn to create and destroy in an infinite cycle. Kali, through tandava, expresses the creativity of chaos.

Every literal and metaphorical image of Kali is thus laden with spiritual import; meditation on the symbolism of the Goddess has the power to transform her devotees.

---

*The *kancukas* are the five coverings of *maya* (the beginningless cause that brings about the illusion of the world): limitation of time, limitation of place, limitation of attachment, limitation of knowledge, the impression of limited creativity.

The Kaula Tradition

*T*he Kaula tradition, which originated in Assam (a state in northeast India), migrated toward Kashmir in the northwest in several waves starting in the fourth century, a time at which we find the first written traces of the *Vijnanabhairava Tantra*,* a key text of Kashmiri Shaivism.† *Kaula* refers to Shiva/Shakti. From their union is born the Kaula path. It's the realization that the union of Bhairava and Bhairavi is the ultimate consciousness, the heart. *Kaula* also means "family" or "group" of practitioners.

It seems that the first two masters who taught in

---

*In the form of a discourse between the god Shiva and his consort Shakti, the *Vijnanabhairava Tantra* briefly presents 112 meditation methods or centering techniques.[1]

†According to David Peter Lawrence in the Internet Encyclopedia of Philosophy (www.iep.utm.edu/kashmiri), "What is commonly called 'Kashmiri Shaivism' is actually a group of several monistic and tantric religious traditions that flourished in Kashmir from the latter centuries of the first millennium C.E. through the early centuries of the second."

Kashmir were named Isvarashiva and Sankararasi. The Kaula path was expounded upon in a masterful way by the Mahasiddha Matsyendranath, and it was not long before Kali became the creative feminine—that from which all else began.

BIRTH OF THE KAULA PATH

The legendary birth of the Kaula path is attributed to Matsyendranath, who received it directly from Shiva. The tale relates that in order to hear a secret teaching that Shiva was giving to Parvati at the ocean's edge, Matsyendranath changed himself into a fish. And this is how he got his name: *matsyendra* means "fish," and *nath* means "lord." He approached the couple and was able to gather together the whole teaching of the Kaula path, which he subsequently transmitted to Kashmir and to others all along the tantric road leading through Nepal to Kashmir. The Kaula tradition went on to play a central role in Kashmiri Shaivism and the practices of Kali. Matsyendranath later died in Nepal, in the valley of Kathmandu, where his memory is still celebrated today.

Matsyendranath's original voyage to Kashmir, accomplished over several years, took the same route that the Kashmiri masters used when traveling to teach in Assam. They made pilgrimages to Kamakya, the location of the temple of the yoni of the Goddess. The yoni of the Goddess fell there, near the Brahmaputra River, when her body was dismembered by Vishnu. He did this to liberate the gods from the horrifying cries of Shiva, who was carrying the body of

Shakti through space. The body—cut into fifty pieces—fell onto the land of India, and each piece was the origin of a sacred site (*pitha*). The fifty pieces represent the fifty syllables of the Sanskrit language. For this reason, in the ritual of rendering the body sacred—which precedes the sexual ritual of the Sacred Union—these fifty sacred sites are indicated on the body of the initiate using a ritual touch.

In the tradition there is another version of the birth of the Kaula path. It relates to the sage Vashistha who, having practiced yogic austerities for many years, had not managed to attain *siddhis,* or special powers. One night he had a dream that entreated him to travel up the Brahmaputra River to its source. He was assured that there he would find a kingdom inhabited by wise beings and receive his final teaching. He set out, traveled upriver, crossed Mahacina, or Great China (Tibet, perhaps), and finally discovered the kingdom of the wise. To his great astonishment he saw that the masters—among whom was Vishnu in an incarnation of Buddha who preceded the historical Buddha—were playing and taking full advantage of the pleasures of life: music and dance, nudity, wine, indulgence of the senses, poetry, and divine orgies.

Vashistha received the teaching of the Kaula path, which swept away his prejudices and freed him from many long years of controlling the senses, which he had imposed in vain. He received the rituals, the practices, the worldview, and instruction in the use of the five "M"s: *madya* (wine), *mamsa* (meat), *matsya* (fish), *mudra* (grains), and *maithuna* (sexual union). In following these teachings, Vashistha quickly attained complete enlightenment. He went back down to Kamakya and began to teach the Kaula path. The principal outlines of this teaching can be summarized as follows:

- Complete freedom from rules and rituals.
- All practices—ritual bath, mantras, chanting, ceremonies—are done mentally.
- No rules in relation to auspicious moments in time— any moment is just fine.
- Nothing is pure or impure.
- No dietary restrictions.
- Women must be worshipped and respected as incarnations of the Goddess.

For us not to be lost in chronologies or in the appearance of individuals, such as in the story of Vashistha, who met a Buddha, it is important to understand that India does not share our sense of time, and tantric practitioners share it even less so. We can see, for example, that in the lineage of Matsyendranath he and his disciple Gorakshanath seem to be separated from each other by a full century or even two. This can seem strange for a Westerner but causes not the slightest problem for a tantric practitioner, because Kali devours time!

After centuries of evolution of the teachings in Kashmir, they were given clear expression by Abhinavagupta (ca. 950–1020 CE), widely recognized as one of the greatest philosophers of South Asia. He was born in the Valley of Kashmir into a brahmin family of scholars and mystics. A musician, poet, dramatist, and theologian, he had a profound influence on Indian culture. After receiving initiation in the Kaula path from his master Sambhunatha, Abhinavagupta achieved enlightenment. In his long life he completed more than thirty-five works, the largest and most famous of which is *Tantraloka,* an encyclopedic treatise on all the philosophical and practical aspects of the Kaula tradition. Abhinavagupta renders homage to Matsyendranath at the beginning of this work.

KAULA TEXTS

The most difficult aspect of dating the composition of tantric scriptures (known as *tantras*), and what actually makes all dating of them impossible, is the existence of the oral tradition. A text that is considered to be the first appearance of a Tantra can in fact come from a source that antedates it by several centuries. Western researchers ferret out the most ancient texts. However, yogis have always functioned with oral transmission, the spoken word. This oral transmission is considered much more reliable, because it takes place within the strict framework of initiation. The scholars, on the other hand, like to add their own contribution to the writing and translation of texts, which renders them less reliable.

Kaula Upanishad
The *Kaula Upanishad,* a short text, gives a condensed version of the Kaula worldview. This view was expanded indefinitely as it migrated to Kashmir and encountered the cosmic worldview of Abhinavagupta, his masters, and his disciples.

The five objects of the senses are the cosmos in expansion.
The undivided Absolute is the Creator.
Ignorance is identical to knowledge.

Lord Ishvara is the cosmos.

The eternal is identical to the ephemeral.

The absence of dharma (righteousness) is dharma.

The five links form the essence of true knowing.

Of all the senses, the eye is king!

In your behavior do the opposite to what the norms dictate
but remain in consciousness.

Freedom is not to be found in knowledge.

Don't make distinctions.

Don't speak of things with pashus (limited beings).

Give up pride.

The Guru is unity.

Do not condemn other practices.

Take no vow.

Impose no restriction on yourself.

Limiting yourself does not lead to freedom.

Practice innerly.

This is freedom.

May the Kaula path triumph!

Kularnava Tantra

Composed around the year 1000, the *Kularnava Tantra* provides the most complete definition of the central approach
for understanding the Kaula tradition as the Royal Road of
Shakti, which abolishes the dichotomy between renunciation
and enjoyment. It is also the vira path: the tantric hero way.

The *Kularnava Tantra* says: "No doctrine, no path can
really compare with this Sun of Kaula."[2] But this nondual
way is only for valorous aspirants: "You can walk along the
sharp edge of a sword, catch a tiger by his neck, carry a ser-

pent on your body, but following the Kaula path is much more difficult."

In the *Kularnava Tantra* value systems are turned upside down—a point of view that is rejected by the external world but prized on the Kaula path. There is neither merit nor demerit, neither good nor bad, neither paradise nor hell. This approach helps the Kaula hero (*vira*) gain freedom from the limitations of a thinking that imposes dualism. Whoever devotes himself to this sadhana becomes Bhairava/Bhairavi (or Shiva/Shakti), on the condition that he frees himself from doubt, fear, and duality.

The *Kularnava Tantra* relates that there are three forms of initiation: by touch, by voice, by spirit. All three are without a definite form, without ritual. The disciple receives grace through contact with Shakti.

The aspirant must be "pure of heart, supremely joyous," devoid of anger and associative thoughts. He rejects inferior rituals; he is kindly and worships the lineage of the masters. He is generous and full of devotion. He supports the brotherhood of gurus. He practices formless meditation—*samadhi*.

Following this path, a yogi feels at ease in any place and under any circumstance. The yogi plays like a child; he has no image to defend, nothing to justify. He is free of the judgment of others.

THE THIRTY-SIX TATTVAS

The body itself is the temple in the Kaula tradition. Within it are to be found the thirty-six tattvas, or categories, which extend all the way from the base to the Absolute beyond

Shiva/Shakti.* Therefore, it is not necessary to reject the body or abandon it to know union with the Divine; on the contrary, one must dissolve it into the cosmos, rendering it similar to earth, water, fire, air, and ether. This practice awakens and brings vibration (*spanda*)† to the body, which becomes aware that it *is* the cosmos.

The Thirty-six Tattvas

Five Elements	Earth	Water	Fire	Air	Space
Five Sense Impressions	Odor	Taste	Sight	Touch	Sound
Five Sense Organs	Nose	Tongue	Eye	Skin	Ear
Five Organs of Action	Excretion	Creation	Motion/Foot	Grasping/Hand	Speaking/Mouth
Five Aspects of the Empirical Individual	Nature	Mind	Ego	Intellect	Spirit
Five Limitations of Maya	Space	Time	Attachment	Knowledge	Power
Five Verities	Illusion of individuality	Subjectivity invested as power in action	Awareness of one's absolute nature	Shiva	Shakti
The Thirty-sixth Tattva	Beyond Shiva/Shakti				

It is essential to understand that the last tattva, the Absolute, or the Divine, is present in each of the other tattvas and that even the base elements—earth, water, fire, air, and

---

*For a detailed description of the tattvas see the teaching of Lalita Devi in my book *Tantric Quest: An Encounter with Absolute Love,* Inner Traditions, 1997.

† *Spanda* means "continuous vibration."

ether—are saturated with the Divine. Therefore, there is no movement forward except in full awareness that all manifestation is divine.

KALI AND SHIVA

Kali (Shakti) and Shiva are united in the same body and in the same knowledge, but when they separate they experience passion. Kali defies Shiva in the ecstatic dance of tandava (dance of creation and dissolution). She wins, leaving Shiva exhausted. Their sexuality is also the expression of a combat in which Kali always assumes the dominant position (*viparita*). Shiva allows Kali to whirl on his lingam until ecstasy is reached. Their separation into two distinct bodies also gives birth to the sixty-four Tantras based on their dialogues, which is the usual form of these texts, some taught by Shakti, others by Shiva.

THE KASHMIRI VISION OF YOGA, TANDAVA, AND THE PRACTICES OF KALI

To properly understand Abhinavagupta's interest in Kali, about which he wrote a great deal, it is important to understand that from the Kashmiri perspective yoga is not at all what is usually taught in the West or in India. Yoga is a being's leap toward recognition of the Self, a mystical realization that goes far beyond what is typically understood by *yoga*. Lilian Silburn explains this clearly in her introduction to Abhinavagupta's text on the twelve Kalis.

From beginning to end, the way of energy is essentially mystical. Consequently, the means for liberation advocated by the philosophers and ascetics of India—doing yoga, self-restraint, discipline, postures—represent only an external deployment involving the breath, the body, and thought. Since these means do not connect in an immediate way with Reality, they cannot lead to an awareness of Reality. . . . We shall see that the practice of the twelve Kalis leads to the spontaneous worship called Supreme Heart, a pure and vibrational Act (*spanda*). It is vague because everything flows without preparation of the body, or of the attention, or of the breath, or of the spoken word. One need only then remain in an immutable way in Reality without concerning oneself about restrictions regarding purity, impurity or any other limitation; none of these are relevant once Supreme Consciousness has been penetrated.[3]

The *Kularnava Tantra* also insists on the fact that the practices typically associated with yoga, such as *asanas* (postures), *pranayama* (breath control), and the austerities, are not part of tantric practice. The only physical exercise that is practiced—in conformity with the *Vijnanabhairava Tantra* and with ancient texts and iconography—consists of the slow dance of tandava followed by a sudden stopping of movement. To avoid different interpretations, including my own, there is nothing better than to return to the Sanskrit words in the text as published by Swami Satyasangananda Saraswati of the Bihar School of Yoga.

Having been placed thus, turn the body slowly. As a result
of this movement, in calmness, in spirit, O Goddess,
the Divine, flooding in, culminates. (*Vijnanabhairava
Tantra,* stanza 83)

Turning, the body, and suddenly, falling down, on the
ground, cessation of energy, which causes disturbance,
there appears, Supreme Energy. (*Vijnanabhairava Tantra,*
stanza 111)[4]

In his commentary, the author makes clear that he is
speaking of tandava.

This method was used by mystics of the Sufi tradition in
order to achieve elevated states of ecstasy and trance and
to attain union with the Divine. Shiva's dance of destruction, *Tandav nritya,* during which Shiva turned without
stopping until the whole universe began to resonate with
the vibration of this dance is a valid illustration of this
dharana.[5]

Most Western commentators, except for Attilia Sironi in
his magnificent Italian translation, ignore this reference to
the dance of tandava. Sironi puts it as follows:

When you allow your body to move slowly in the dance,
it can happen, O Goddess,
that the nature of mind becomes calm
and it is then that we receive
a flooding in of the Divine.

And:

> After having spun around one's
> axis for a long time,
> it is thanks to a sudden fall to the ground
> that the Supreme State becomes present
> since the power of disturbance
> has been stopped.[6]

In Kashmiri yoga there is no notion of the void but instead a notion of space since—in order to apprehend the Reality that Abhinavagupta speaks about—it is essential to understand the world as a reality. The idea of illusion brought by Hinduism and by Buddhism, and which amounts to an impulse of negation of the real, finds no echo in the Kashmiri masters. In speaking of "body/space" or "cosmic body," it is clear that space encompasses all tangible reality, including the body, which itself includes the cosmos. However, there is in Buddhism and in Hinduism a very powerful logic: in renouncing the world and seeing it as an illusion, the body is then devalued and seen as a "bag of excrement."

As Alain Daniélou remarks with a touch of humor, "It is difficult, it would seem, for those in India to completely leave behind the Puritan morality that they have adopted—they really believe that you can live an ideal life with this kind of limitation."[7] This explains the often unbridgeable divide that exists between Hinduism and Tantrism—a divide so great that one dares hardly even to speak of Tantra in India where stories about tantric practitioners circulate that are similar to those about witches in the Middle Ages in Europe.

If, on the other hand, it's a matter of being fully alive, let us move on toward all that sets us vibrating, refusing nothing, leaving behind austerities that dry us out, and instead let us see the reality of the world. This major difference explains why Abhinavagupta, who played the great *vina* (a stringed instrument), had such an admiration for music and for the arts, which set us vibrating, revealing spanda.

This vision of Reality is founded on the certitude that only that which manifests in consciousness exists. All matter from the elements up to Shiva/Shakti and the thirty-sixth tattva, even beyond Shiva/Shakti, is infused with Supreme Consciousness. There is nothing then that is vile, material, subtle, divine. No more separation. Kali then becomes the supreme energy of Shiva—the wheel of energies can manifest.

> A yogi who is attentive to the circle of the radiation of his own power and who oversees the activation of his sense organs as well as their stability along with other functions, must consider his own essence like that of the Lord, like that which directs and incites functions and organs toward their respective objects. He will then possess everywhere the spontaneous freedom of his real nature, which allows him to obtain this vibrant Act.[8]

3

Preliminary Practices of the Kaula Tradition

*I*n the Kaula tradition the place of the guru (spiritual teacher) is fundamental, and to fully enjoy this connection you must not only abandon yourself to him or her but also communicate with the whole lineage of the Spanda Way and the Pratyabhijna Way, which are united, according to Abhinavagupta and Lalita Devi, and which are considered to be direct emanations of Kaula. The yoga of the lineage is indispensable so that the practitioner is linked to both his master and to the tradition. There are several versions of this yoga; we provide the most complete one here.

❖ The Yoga of the Lineage
This yoga of the lineage must be done slowly, in great concentration. It is the most important stage of the tantric sadhana. It alone permits union with the master and the lineage.

1. In a state of intense collectedness, imagine the universe in the infinity of its spatial nature and identify your own

consciousness with it while reciting inwardly the mantra *AUM*.

2. Then, slowly, imagine that the universe shrinks and dissolves into the globe of the earth, and then that the earth itself dissolves into the place where you are located.

3. Recite the root mantra (*AUM*) once more and reabsorb the vision of the location in space that is around you. As you float in this way in space, visualize your master facing you and close enough that you can feel the quivering vibration of Shakti present in him.* Feel that it makes you vibrate like a well-tuned instrument.

4. In the gentle intensity of this state of vibration, address him as follows:

   "Oh master, you who are the culminating result of the lineage of yoginis and yogis of Kaula and of the Spanda and Pratyabhijna paths—paths of the spontaneous recognition of the Self—you are charged in this instant with all the skill of those who have transmitted the secret knowledge and the yoga of the spirit."

5. Repeat this invocation three times, and when you say for the last time "you are charged in this instant with all the skill of those who have transmitted the secret knowledge and the yoga of the spirit," see suddenly appear in the space around your master all the *siddhas*† of the lineage, both yogi and yogini. From their adamantine bodies rays of light converge toward your master, whose human body transforms into a diamond. All his human imperfections

---

*For clarity's sake, the practice is described here with the master being a male but can certainly be adapted to refer to a female guru.

†*Siddhas* are "perfected ones," those who have attained spiritual liberation.

disappear while he becomes Shiva/Shakti in androgynous form.

6. When your master becomes only an adamantine form floating in the light, all the siddhas of the lineage dissolve into him and his luminosity increases even more.

7. At this moment, an intense point of adamantine light the size of a grain of mustard seed shines forth from the center between the eyebrows of your master, striking the corresponding center in you. This source of luminosity gradually fills your body as if it were a vase, your skin being the outline of its shape. Little by little, your organs, your feelings, your concepts, your emotions become as if liquefied into pure love, dissolving the associative mind. You are now nothing more than vibration and light. Your body loses all specificity and becomes adamantine like that of your master whom you are facing in the midnight blue of space.

8. Then from the throat center of your master there appears a very intense red luminous point, and the rays from it strike your throat. This light purifies your voice, which now becomes simply spanda, "the song of quivering vibration."

9. Finally, from the heart center of your master, there appears a blue point. Its rays come vibrating toward your heart, which opens and welcomes the light and the feeling of more spaciousness. All sense of ego has been completely abandoned.

10. Breathe out forcefully, sending out the last traces of darkness, of blame, and of doubt that might still remain in you.

11. Maintaining an awareness of your breathing, starting from your own heart and reaching out to the heart of your

master, breathe out gently in a harmonious half-circular movement. Then, from the heart of your master and reaching to your own heart, breathe in gently in a harmonious half circle, forming in this way a perfect circle in space.

12. At this instant, you hear the voice of your master saying to you:

> [Your name], noble daughter [son] of the Pratyabhijna and Spanda lineages, through this yoga realize that we are united in the same knowing and in the same body. When your adamantine body approaches and merges with mine, when my lingam [my yoni] of diamond penetrates your yoni [absorbs your lingam] of crystal, and when a flood of luminous pleasure passes through our bodies in a slow and voluptuous circle following our breathing, our supreme essences, the sap of our subtle essences intimately linked voyages through space. This sap rises up from your yoni [lingam], makes joyful the navel and the heart, delights the throat, fills the mouth with the taste of paradise and through your lips comes to drink me up. Traversing my body in a downward movement, our ambrosia attains the supreme state and as it penetrates once again, it takes sustenance once again.
>
> One thousand times this flood traverses us, and little by little we dissolve in subtle climactic pleasure. Bhairava/Bhairavi are forming now a river of invisible, vibrating light that spirals into space and suddenly fills the totality of all worlds.

13. If you attain the state of nonduality with your master, remain in that state as long as possible.

When you leave it, thank your master and the lineage for the grace that they have accorded you in the descent of energy from Shakti (Shaktipata) and meditate as it seems pleasurably right for you.

This constitutes the secret practice of the Yoga of the Lineage, as it was given to the noble daughters and noble sons of the lineages of Kaula, Pratyabhijna, and Spanda, having overcome the obstacle of doubt and having set out with determination on the path of the supreme recognition of the Self in quivering vibration.

> *Homage to the yoginis and yogis of the lineages of Kaula, Pratyabhijna, and Spanda who have transmitted this yoga so that beings might attain identification with the masters and attain the marvelous Bhairavi state.* *

❖ The Yoga of the Five Elements

The yoga of the five elements (five of the thirty-six tattvas) is the beginning of the transformation of the ordinary body into a cosmic body. This practice transforms the yogi into the five elements: earth, water, fire, wind, and ether, or space. It stabilizes the spirit, destroys poisons and egoism, and makes consciousness known. This practice allows reality to be conquered.

---

*Bhairavi and Bhairava are the secret, nocturnal, mysterious aspects of Shakti and Shiva, representing pure consciousness. They are invoked between 3:00 a.m. and 5:00 a.m., which sets the mood for this period of the night.

⬧ Earth

The yogi meditates on his body as being a square floating in midnight blue space. Little by little his body transforms into liquid gold. He glows in space and vanquishes illness. After three years of this practice, the body becomes adamantine; he is inhabited by the strength of nine elephants and enters into continuous vibration (spanda). Breathing stabilizes in the heart. The yoga contemplates himself as Shiva residing in his heart and illuminating his body with his own radiance. He is seated on a black lotus. He spreads his luminosity around the world and becomes one with the element earth.

⬧ Water

The yogi visualizes himself floating in midnight blue space. His body has a half-moon shape. A white lotus is positioned at his throat. The yogi imagines his body fresh as the full moon and immersed in water. He thinks, "There is nothing else either in me or outside of me." His body liquefies; his appearance becomes like water. His body rises above the water. He masters illness, becoming water. He is filled with a lunar glow arising from the lotus at his throat. He becomes one with the element water.

⬧ Fire

The yogi contemplates his body as a triangle surrounded by a belt of fire. A burning emerges from his body and burns everything outside it. Illness departs from him. After a season of practice, he can turn whatever he touches to flames. He enters into vibration. He is the spirit of fire. He contemplates himself in his human form. He meditates on his palate, which produces a sparking fire surrounded by smoke like the sun in a cloud of smoke. In this way he becomes the element fire and masters the mantras. He spreads his light over the world and experiences the tranquillity of Shiva.

✦ Wind

The yogi visualizes himself as a midnight blue sphere in which six drops of a lighter blue are floating. The drops vibrate and produce a sound. He frees himself from illness. He can cover great distances without tiring and can take the form of the wind. He visualizes his body as midnight blue. He becomes the tattva of the wind by visualizing himself as a sparking sapphire. He becomes unfathomable.

✦ Ether

The yogi begins to visualize his midnight blue body, which becomes transparent little by little until it becomes ether. The yogi experiences the sensation of more spaciousness. He becomes immune to the venom of serpents. He is freed from illness. He becomes space and can pass through elements. He becomes invisible and sees the earth as porous. He can become the emptiness of a dark, rocky cavity. He visualizes ether positioned at his forehead. He contemplates himself as the moon devoured by the eclipse and becomes Shiva, the lord of mantras.

PREPARATORY VISUALIZATIONS

Preliminary practices are necessary to accustom us to Kali, to her revelatory power that will plumb the depths of our subconscious until it reaches the wellspring of life. Kali brings us directly face to face with death. She reveals and authorizes our violence in a ritual framework, which has the effect of considerably calming our impulses. This latent violence is precisely what we don't know what to do with in most of our spiritual approaches. In Kali we have a direct, extreme, and healthy approach.

❖ Deep Relaxation of the Corpse

It is not advisable to do this practice alone the first few times that you engage in it.

1. Lie comfortably stretched out on the ground, if possible in direct contact with the earth itself, in a forest or a place far from human habitation. Concentrate on the breath and breathe in as you relax fully the deep muscles of the belly just above the pubic bone. As you breathe out, allow these muscles to move back into position. Let the spine participate in this movement: a breathing that moves through the whole body and connects it to the cosmos.

2. Then imagine that you are dead and that a great feeling of peace comes into you. You are being reconnected to nature. Become one with everything. Little by little, your body decomposes.

   Pieces of flesh, muscles, organs separate from the bone and fall to the ground, which welcomes them. In this return to the elements there is a veritable voluptuousness that needs to be savored, because the very idea of death terrifies us, whereas the experience can be felt as a grand return to nature.

3. The earth absorbs the pieces of flesh. The bones appear as a beautiful whiteness. And from the effects of wind, sun,

and weather, the pieces break apart and are ground into a powder that mixes with the earth until you have completely disappeared into the voluptuousness of a return to unity.

4. After having enjoyed this state for an extended moment, imagine that all the cells of the flesh come back together, vivified by the earth; they re-form muscles and organs, which reattach themselves to the skeleton, which also is reassembled. But take note that in this return to life there is a tranquil space that the body previously lacked—an organic pleasure that has been washed free of its memories, a new freshness, a harmonious and delicious functioning.

5. Begin to gently move your arms, your legs, your head, your hips, your torso as if you were dancing the tandava lying down.

6. Return to the seated position and meditate for a moment to accustom yourself to your harmonized body, now reconnected to the nature with which it is now blended. It is as if there is no longer any difference between your body and the environment. You are one with everything.

❖ The Obsidian Grotto of the Fifty Kalis

1. Imagine that you are seated in smallish obsidian grotto, as if you were in a womb of shiny blackness. There is not the slightest ray of light. The temperature is pleasant. Through your presence and in your breathing, you let your body communicate with the complete darkness until the moment when you feel your sense perceptions shifting. The complete darkness erodes the limits of the senses.

2. After a few hours, you perceive the odor or taste of a sound, you contact an imaginary perception, you see with the skin, and so on.

3. You are naked, the sensitivity of the skin increases, you touch the obsidian, you taste it.

4. An internal movement begins in the rock, like bodies trying to free themselves. Little by little, these bodies emit sounds; in the darkness you see the cleavers of the Kalis emerging out of the obsidian. Arms and legs emerge, tongues of the Kalis point through the rock. Faces. The Kalis dance to free themselves. They emit more and more powerful growls and cries.

5. Finally they break away from the obsidian and leap into the grotto around you, letting fly terrifying howls. They are small, about three feet high. The cleavers emit flashes of light, and, although you are in darkness, you see the shiny teeth, the red tongues, and the eyes of the Kalis in flashes like quick hallucinations that give you no time to see the details.

6. Suddenly the fifty Kalis fall into deep silence. Nothing moves. This is the calm that precedes the attack.

7. All the Kalis throw themselves upon you and cut you into pieces that lie scattered on the ground.

8. The Kalis throw down their cleavers, crouch down, and eat your cut-up body. You disappear.

9. The Kalis disappear.

10. The grotto disappears.

11. Now you are only space.

THE EXPRESSION OF VIOLENCE AND ITS TRANSMUTATION INTO ABSOLUTE LOVE

In this remarkable practice there will not be any transmutation of violence until it is fully exercised. The practice will free the practitioner from the torrent that keeps being held on to and that constitutes a real venom, poisoning human relations. Here, it is not a question of trying to change the violence into its opposite, which will only cover over the problem with an unrealistic dream that we could be full of love. Instead, it's a matter of giving full expression to a dynamic that social taboos always fail to repress: our violence.

This is one of the constants in tantric thought: the solution to a problem lies in the problem. Moving outside it will not set things straight. On the contrary, you must have the courage to penetrate to the heart of the darkness and stop constructing an idealized being who has all the trouble in the world coexisting with deeply human reality. To convince ourselves of this we need only be aware of the number of times where, in a conflict, we have purely and simply imagined getting out of the conflict by wishing for the death of our opponent. If we were suddenly surrounded by all our dead, there would be a great number of bodies. In spite of that, we have not succeeded in eradicating our violence.

Once in the *chan* (zen) tradition in China, there was a master who began violently slapping his potential disciples right from the first interview. One disciple asked for the reason for this welcome. The master replied simply, "You know now that you are a violent being. Instinctively you wished me dead. Starting there we are going to be able to work together. You have seen your reality!"

The visualization that we are presenting here is one of the most beautiful of the Kali practices, because it allows us to understand the inexorable sequence of violence and its liberation in absolute love.

❖ *Kali in the Dark Forest*

1. Imagine that you are Kali. Beautiful. Adolescent, overflowing with untamed power. Your skin is black or midnight blue. Naked, supple, a huntress—all senses on full alert. You brandish your cleaver. You are like a tigress, nose to the wind in order to sniff out the presence of a potential victim.

2. You move through the dark forest with a light step, softly. When you begin to feel your untamed strength mounting you stoke it to incandescence by remembering, one after the other, all those people who have made you suffer in your life. They are going to appear in the forest. The cruelest ones first.

3. As soon as you feel their presence, violence rises up in you, your lips draw back, your power increases, and you run toward your first victim. When your victim sees you, she is stricken with panic. You savor the moment before cutting her to pieces. Each one of your victims merits individual treatment. Some you just slice in two, others get chopped into tiny pieces. As pieces fall to the ground, you stride through them, rushing on to your next victim.

4. The more the trail of victims lengthens, the more your savagery explodes. You control nothing. Pure expression of violence!

    At first you will have some difficulty letting your energy explode, but little by little, just like the mythological Kali, you are swept along.

5. A moment will come when you have killed all those who hurt you, and you will feel the energy begin to swing back.

    At that moment, you leave the dark forest and discover

a very beautiful valley. It's nighttime with stars and moon-light, the Himalayas, and a beautiful lake. The placid surface of the lake attracts you, and you walk toward it. Your body becomes calm.

6. You arrive near the lake and, slipping into the cool water, all traces of blood are washed away. Sweetness over-comes you little by little. You drop your cleaver and begin to feel a deep relaxation in the muscles that were tensed in violence.

7. Your body becomes so light that the energy of the water propels it to the surface. You float, arms and legs crossed, watching with deep happiness the crescent moon, the snowy peaks, the stars. Your breathing becomes soft and subtle. You are in harmony with earth and sky, water and space.

8. Suddenly, among the stars, all the fragments that you cut up appear. They float for a moment in the midnight blue sky and then rain down into the lake. As soon as the body fragments touch the water, they become light and lumi-nous; they float around you like constellations.

9. Little by little the fragments come together and the bodies re-form. You no longer feel the slightest animosity or the slightest tension. The bodies assemble in the same place as you—their feet and hands touching, they form a circle around you. A mandala is created with you at its center. You understand that the beings who made you suffer are victims and that they had no other language available to them. You understand that all violence comes from frustra-tion. You can no longer hold anything against them.

10. On the contrary, such a force of love circulates between

you and them that umbilical cords spring out of your navel and attach you to the navel of each person in this first circle. You nourish them with your love and knock down the transmission of violence. There is not even forgiveness—just understanding of the chain of violence that you have just broken. You have become the Kali of infinite love.

11. Once you understand that your aggressors are victims, a second circle forms, made up of those who brought suffering to those who were violent toward you. From the first circle, umbilical cords bring nourishment to the second circle.

12. More circles form. In this way you can create five of them in a magnificent mandala that floats in the midnight blue sky.

   The chain of violence is broken.

This practice is extremely powerful; little by little it eradicates our most violent instincts.

The *Nirrutara Tantra*

Scripture That Is Superior to All Others

*A*fter these preliminary practices, the aspirant, under the guidance of a master, can enter into the central Kali ritual. There are numerous versions and variants in the different Tantras, but the one that is detailed in the *Nirrutara Tantra* is certainly the oldest and most profound. *Nirrutara* means "the one that is superior to all others." This Sanskrit text is translated for the first time into a Western language.*

The Goddess said,

"O God, O God, great God! You who are the essence of the creation, maintenance, and dissolution of the world,

---

*A number of years ago a Sanskrit scholar who was attending some weekend seminars in Paris gave me her French translation of the *Nirrutara Tantra,* but she unfortunately forgot to add her name to the manuscript that she left with me. I hope that she will contact me so that I can include her name in the next edition. I thank her with all my heart for her remarkable work.

what is the nature of the Dakshina Kali, and what is
the nature of her mantra?

"Or as well what worship is to be made to her and what is the
benefit of such worship? Or what master will guide us,
O God? And what initial discipline is to be observed?

"What evocation of the Goddess ought to be made, and
what benefit can be derived from that?

"Explain all this to me in an exhaustive way, so that I no
longer have questions."

Lord Shiva replied:

"The Blessed Dakshina, Mistress of the three *gunas*
[qualities] must be understood as the womb.

"Everything that exists, animate and inanimate, is of the
nature of the womb, O Mistress of the Kula [Kula =
Kaula].

"O you who transmit Sacred Knowledge, you the Goddess,
you are considered to be 'all that is.' This is so in three
aspects: Kali knows the art of emitting abundantly the
sound HA, she is of subtle essence, and she appears in
the form of the center of the yoni.

"And the yoni is Dakshina Kali, the very essence of Shiva,
Vishnu, and Brahma.

"And in the triangle are to be found the three gods: Shiva,
Vishnu, and Brahma.

"In the center of the yoni, O Goddess, must there tarry the
goddess Kalika, the Beautiful One of Maha-Kali in
her form of light—she of resplendent beauty, she who
brings all manifestation into the world.*

---

*Kalika and Maha-Kali are both variants of the name Kali.

"From this light the universe is born. From the fact of the separation of Shiva and Shakti, Shiva and Shakti appear in two ways, O Goddess. They are devoid of attributes while gifted with all attributes.

"Without attributes, she is a multitude of lights. She has the eternity of Para-Brahman [the highest Absolute]. O you who are like the highest Purusha [Spirit]. O you who have the highest splendor of sapphire.

"And the Dakshina Kali, who is light, may be very distant when she manifests diversity. When she is in the amorous union of *viparitarata* [active, in top position], Kali is without attributes although gifted with attributes.

"She can also be, O you who are without attributes, Aniruddha Sarasvati [Aniruddha means "without limitations"].

"And when she is gifted with attributes, O daughter of the gods, she takes the form of Maha-Kala.

"As soon as she assumes the form of a woman, the world is engendered. The great Lakshmi, the Maya of Vishnu, maintains the world in illusion.

"In the path of the yoni, this Goddess, whether or not she is provided with attributes, is all that is inanimate and animate.

"This world is a divine way. It is used as a way toward the Divine.

"The original principle made up of Shiva/Shakti is the initial cause of the knowledge of principles.

"Upon the completion of numerous existences, knowledge of Shakti is engendered.

"Without the knowledge of Shakti, O Goddess, supreme
　　deliverance cannot take place.

"The Shakti Dakshina Kali is the very essence of the science
　　of attainment.

"According to all traditions of attainment, Dakshina is Spirit
　　and Nature. The one and the other are in a reciprocal
　　relationship of nonseparation.

"If Shiva himself is legitimate, Shakti must be, through the
　　fact of her union with Shiva.

"The principle corresponding to the united Shiva/Shakti is
　　invoked as a result of their union.

"The mantra corresponding to this union must be uttered
　　by invoking the union of the two of them. The mantra
　　of the two of them is the Great Mantra that bestows
　　pleasure and liberation from the world.

"Through this pleasure, you obtain fourfold deliverance,
　　from the fact of belonging to the world, and so on.

"Kali is the fabled tree that satisfies all desire. She is
　　Aniruddha Sarasvati.

"On the level of the great gods—Brahma, Vishnu, and Shiva
　　the Supreme Lord—the sole cause of the pleasure and
　　liberation from the world is the Goddess Kali, which
　　cannot be divorced from the fact of her importance. She
　　is the very essence of mantra and tantra.

"I am going to speak now, O Sovereign of Kula, of
　　humankind and of the Dakshina Kali. The liberated-
　　alive is engendered by this knowledge alone,
　　accompanied by a practice of meditation, O Goddess,
　　fully associated with the *nada* [vibrating hum] and the
　　bindu, combined with the flow of the left eye.

"In the practice of the path of the left hand, consciousness
by its very essence is absolute and relative.

"She is unique and supreme divinity, sovereign of the mantra
and of the science of attainment, O Mistress of the
Kula.

"She is gifted with the three qualities, at the crossroads
of illusion, at the crossroads of propriety, and then
supreme.

"Once you have placed the Dakshina Kali in your heart, you
must direct her mind to the seven source-elements [*bija*].

"Based on the fact that you had to consecrate her innerly
as the spouse of Fire, she is proclaimed Queen of
Knowledge.

"She is mistress of all the mantras. She is knowledge.
She is the one who gives rise to the creation and the
destruction of the world—regardless of whether she is a
woman like you or a man like me.

"Therefore her mantra is identical to Aniruddha Sarasvati.
All the gods—Brahma, Rudra, Vishnu—are at her
service.

"In the Vedas, the Agamas, and the Puranas, Kalika is
revered for her beauty. In the land of Kama [god of
love], she is the one who satisfies all passions.

"Certain ones who are Bhairavas [fearless] in heaven, are
all sons of Kalika in the human realm or in the lower
worlds. Without a doubt, they are liberated here in our
lower realm.

"Because of the difficulty of the path, O Queen of the Gods,
initiation does not take place following the direction of
a master.

"Similarly, at the moment of the ritual especially, you need
   to send away anyone whose awareness is not open.

"On this path, Bhairava is proclaimed the *rishi* [guide], and
   the words intoned are in the Vedic meter *ushnik*.

"And the divinity is the Dakshina Kali as Aniruddha
   Sarasvati.

"And Shakti holds the seed syllables *HRIM, HUM,* and
   KRIM that you designate precisely as the worshipper.

"In the three domains of the pursuit of *dharma*
   [righteousness], *kama* [pleasure, sensual desire], and
   moksha [liberation], their use is recommended.

"Formerly, the multitude of *nyasas* [consecration of the
   various parts of the body through contact] was taught
   in the various Tantras, O Parvati.

"The person officiating in the practice of this multitude of
   nyasas should practice with heroes.

"Among the fifty sacred sites [*pithas*] consecrated on the
   body, the positioning of the yoni must be honored."

੪   ੪

"You must contemplate Kali as languid, her breasts swollen
   with milk, and firm.

"She displays the splendor of storm clouds. She is black. She
   has four arms and lets fly terrifying cries.

"Her lotuslike hands brandish, on the left side, a sword in the
   upper hand and a freshly severed head in the lower hand.

"On the right side, her hand directed upward assumes the
   gesture of eliminating fear and the one pointing down
   assumes the gesture of fulfilling desires. She is covered
   with blood flowing from the garland of severed heads of
   the fifty letters.

"Her mouth is glistening from the river of blood that flows
from her parted lips. She is accompanied by jackals
whose terrifying cries echo in all four directions.

"Her belt is fashioned from a multitude of severed arms. Her
face is smiling. She is naked, cloaked in space. Her hair
flows freely and a half moon is her tiara.

"She is standing on the heart of Mahadeva, who assumes the
form of a cadaver.

"She greedily wants to unite with Mahakala in the dominant
position [viparitarata].

"She writhes from the effects of drunkenness, and the lotus
of her face is radiant. With great violence she laughs in
bursts. Ceaselessly she garners pleasure unto herself."

༵ ༵

"This is how Kali must be viewed. She haunts cremation
grounds. After you have contemplated her like this, the
vira must honor her with a nighttime sacrifice in the
temple of the Kula.

"After having carried out this homage in the mind, you must
collect flowers.

"If the homage is not done mentally, then you have to go to
the field of ancestors.

"Anyone who is deeply vile must absolutely not sacrifice to
Kali, who is the destroyer of impurities.

"The mantra should not be uttered aloud but recited in the
mind with an inner smile.

"And in this case, no sacrifice leads to Kamakhya, O
Mistress of the Kula!

"After having worshipped the divinity innerly with devotion,
an external ritual must be conducted."

※ ※

"After having conducted the purification rites for oneself
and the objects used in worship, you must set out the
vases. The vases for water and so on must be set out
following the regulations.

"In carrying out the sacred site [pitha] ritual, you are
honoring the divinity. You must focus your mind with
supreme devotion, helped by the prescribed rites.

"You lay out in their proper place: water for washing the
feet, purification water, drinking water, ablution water,
the brahmanic cord, the vestment garments, as well
as the totality of ornaments. Then, fragrant flowers,
incense, oil lamps, and honey too.

"Only afterward, after having uttered the mantra, can you
satisfy the divinity by making these offerings to her.

"And then garlands, salves, and the five flowers accompanied
by salutations with hands together at the forehead.

"Once again the Goddess Lalita must be honored by
Maha-Kala.

"Provided with an offering of sixteen objects, this ritual
carries the name of *eight*. It is appreciated by the eight
Shaktis as well as the guardians of worlds.

"This sacrifice, which is carried out gradually from the
sacred site up to the mantra, is taught as the superior
path, beyond all sacred site rituals. It is done in secret."

※ ※

"The ritual to be conducted first is the ritual of the mantra.
The daily ritual must be conducted second.

"As for the ceremony of flowers, it must be done only last
of all.

"Then, after having lifted the veil, Ajna [the chakra between
the brows] must be honored. And Kamala [Lakshmi]
must be honored as well by placing the tiara above the
ear locks.

"And then the group of five masters, O Goddess. And, in
finishing, Maha-Kala, whose color is dark and who
wears his mass of hair tied in a bun, O most dear
Goddess!

"He has three eyes, and in his manifestation as a cadaver he
unites with his Shakti, in ecstasy. Naked, terrible to
look upon, he shines like blue antimony.

"Without attribute and receptacle of all attributes, he is the
place where Kali resides unceasingly. Kali, decorated
with skulls, is the Goddess who positions herself on the
central triangle.

"The goddesses confined to their material images are on the
fifth triangle. They must be honored passionately in
the eight divisions of space successively, beginning
with the east.

"Brahmi and Narayani too, and Kaumari, Maheshvari,
Aparajita, and Chamunda, Varahi, and
Narasimhika.*

"At the four doorways you must honor the Bhairavas, O
Goddess, beginning with the one with the dark body,
Asitanga, then Ruru, Chanda, and Krodha, and
Bhishana as well.

"And Unmatta, Kapali, and Samharaka are invoked in this

---

*As we shall see farther on in the section devoted to the Eight Red God-
desses of Matsyendranath, the names of the Goddess vary from one Tantra
to another.

order. Two by two at each doorway beginning with the east, O Goddess.

"The ten guardians of the celestial realms beginning with Indra must be honored in the ten directions. Homage must be rendered to the sword and to the severed head held in the left hands, O Beautiful One of the Kula.

"The mudras of bestowing gifts and calming fear with the right hands must be honored as well. And once again, the Goddess accompanied by her arms and her mount.

"After mentally invoking Kulluka, she must be represented as a bridge to your heart. You must imagine a great bridge starting at your navel and positioned at your throat.

"This bridge is *pranava* [AUM], O Goddess. It must be honored as being situated in your heart.

"You must represent your own origin as a great bridge positioned at your throat.

"With the *matrikas** united with their bindus [letters connected to their accent marks, or dots]—the mothers united to their centers—they must be visualized connected to the navel. You must represent to yourself the magic of Kali in the illusory form of a young woman, who climaxes in producing the sound *PHAT*.

"You must meditate on the mantra of the five phonemes of Kalika in order to evoke Kulluka. Kulluka is the Goddess Maha-Nila-Sarasvati assuming the form of Tara.

Matrikas can be understood as both the letters of the alphabet and as goddesses.

"And Kulluka is invoked by the same sacred feminine syllables. They must be practiced in the ritual of all those who devote themselves to Kali.

"After having repeated them 108 times, then you can prepare the ritual. Next, the Goddess Lalita must be honored by Maha-Kala. And after that, O Goddess, the hymns and the magic armor [*kavaca*] must be recited."

The Goddess said:

"Lord! Sovereign of all the gods! You who are revered by all beings, explain to me, O God, because it is not clear to me what the magic armor is. If you care for me, do tell me about this, O you who are the most eminent of the gods."

꜀ ꜁

Lord Shiva replied, ["It is as follows]:

"May Siddha-Kali protect your head; may the Dakshina protect your forehead.

"May Kali protect your face constantly; may Kapali protect your eyes.

"May Kulla constantly protect your cheeks and Kuru-Kullika your mouth.

"May Virodhini protect your lips and Vipra-Cittika your chin.

"May Ugra constantly protect your ears, and likewise may Ugra-Prabha protect your nose.

"May Dipta constantly protect your throat, and may Nila-Prabha preserve the nape of your neck.

"May Ghana protect the area of the chest, and may Matra preserve the back ceaselessly.

"May Mudra always protect the navel, and may Mita always
    preserve the phallus.

"May Rati-Priya preserve the base of the phallus and Shiva-
    Priya the yoni.

"In the same way, may Aruna protect the base of the palate
    and Taruna the tongue.

"May Maha-Kala-Priya and Vikata protect respectively the
    knees and the two legs.

"May Shmashana-Vasini protect the spouse and Digambari
    the son. Matta-Hasa, the home, and Sureshvari, the
    mother.

"May Ghora-Rava protect the royal palate, and may Kalika
    stand guard at all times.

"May Ghora-Rupa protect the dharma and Munda-Malini
    the nondharma.

"May Kara-Kanci protect me constantly, and may Kalika
    preserve me at every moment.

"May the three letters of the sacred syllable of Kama protect
    from the navel to the feet. May the two conjoined
    letters of the sacred syllable of Kurca always protect me
    in the areas above the navel.

"May the two letters of the sacred syllable of Shakti
    protect me in addition at the opening at the top of
    the head.

"May the two letters of the sacred syllable of Kama always
    protect me in the direction of the east.

"May the two conjoined letters of the sacred syllable of
    Kurca protect me in the direction of the south and
    preserve me continually.

"May the two conjoined letters of the sacred syllable of

Shakti protect me in the direction of the west, and may
this direction be favorable.

"And may Vahni-Jaya always protect me in the direction of
the north, and may Aniruddha Sarasvati, who governs
knowledge, protect me in all directions."

ꣳ ꣳ

"Prudent is he who carefully intones the magic armor of
Kalika. In truth and beyond all doubt, demons flee
far from her, whether they be *rakshasa, kushmanda,*
phantoms, ghosts, or cannibalistic spirits."

The Goddess asked:

"What praise did Shankara [Shiva] speak, before becoming
the Lord gifted with all powers?

Tell me that, O Lord of the gods, if you care for me."

Lord Shiva replied:

"You who intone the sound *HUM, HUM;* you who are
mounted on a cadaver and whose midnight blue eyes
sparkle;

"You whose face dazzles the three worlds, Homage to you,
Kalika.

"You whose feet we kiss; you who are terrible and you who
wear a garland of severed heads hung around your neck;

"You who are innumerable; you whose belly is of great girth;
you who are fearsome, Homage to you, Kalika.

"You who are a very young girl whose breasts are like an
elephant's forehead bumps; you who govern speech;
you who are kindly and auspicious, Homage to you,
Kalika.

"You who wave your tongue; you who look like Hara [Shiva];
you who bear a triad of eyes;

"Goddess whose bursts of laughter are terrifying, Homage to
  you, Kalika.

"You who are clothed in a tiger skin; you who hold a sword
  in your skillful hand and in the blue lotus of your left
  hand a severed head, Homage to you, Kalika.

"You whose mass of wavy hair is the color of a midnight
  blue lotus; you whose face rises up like a moon with the
  color of red lead; you whose teeth sparkle behind your
  lips, Homage to you Kalika.

"You who bear the color of the smoke of the fires at the
  destruction of the world; you whose eyes are the moon,
  the sun, and fire; you kindly Mother who lives in the
  mountains, Homage to you, Kalika.

"You who receive the torrent of the waters of Brahma and
  Shambu and who stands on the belly of a cadaver; you
  who are accompanied by millions of ghosts, Homage to
  you, Kalika.

"You, destructive Mother full of compassion, you fully
  satisfy all desires;

"You grant all wishes; you procure pleasure; and you bring
  deliverance, Homage to you, Kalika.

"Whoever repeats this praise to Kalika with the deepest
  devotion, once he has completed this task, he will be
  granted magic powers and will no longer need to make
  mental efforts."

5

The Rituals of Kali and the Sacred Union

Numerous rituals support union of the practitioner with the divine Kali, ranging from the chanting of mantras to very complex practices and deep meditations. Kali is beyond rules, so the rituals collected here can be done singly or in any combination.

Although her practices are not linked to any restriction—such as time or place, phase of the moon, astrological configuration, and so on—Kali likes nighttime practice, black moons, Tuesdays, crossroads, deserted places, and cemeteries. She likes red flowers and red clothing, wine, and blood. Sublime essence and sperm intoxicate her with desire.

KALI GAYATRI

The Kali Gayatri mantra* should be chanted 108 times.

---

*A *gayatri* is a Sanskrit song or hymn of three lines of eight syllables each.

OM mahakalyai cha vidmahe
smachan vasinyai cha dhimahi
tanno gore pracodayat

OM. I meditate on the great Goddess who banishes
   darkness.
I contemplate she who resides close to funeral pyres.
May the Goddess open me to total nondual expansion.

A SIMPLE RITUAL OF
CHANTING AND
MAKING OFFERINGS

In this ritual the chanting of certain *bija mantras* (seed syllables) is accompanied by making offerings to the Goddess.
The mantra is chanted 108 times while scattering flower petals and presenting offerings such as incense, spices, water, and
other items—symbolic or real.

OM, HRIM SRIM KRIM Parameshvari Kalike svaha!

The word meanings in English:

OM: the infinite beyond all conception
HRIM: the essence of consciousness, the substance of
   presence
SRIM: expansion beyond all form
KRIM: dissolution in the Absolute
Parameshvari: the supreme Divinity, the great Goddess
Kalike: she who banishes darkness
svaha: I simply become one with the Divine

A KALI VISUALIZATION MEDITATION

Kali is absolute nature, the essence of all the divinities, the great Goddess, consciousness, wonder, and joy. Kali reduces opposing pairs to empty space. She transcends subjugation and liberation. She severs connections. She abolishes the difference between guru and disciple.

In her love game she brings ecstasy and manifests and dissolves formations and worlds. All Tantras arise from her. She is the creator of language. Intimacy with Kali is beyond all knowledge—even revealed scriptures are useless to one who knows her. If she is misunderstood, there is no sadhana that will bear fruit. She is the essence of creation. Manifested as woman, intoxicated by desire, she frees the tantric practitioner from all desire except union with the Divine. In her, the union of guru and disciple is achieved. Her deep nature remains secret.

❖ Kali Visualization

If you contemplate Kali in this form, all darkness, all duality will be destroyed. Time itself will be devoured by the Goddess, who is spirit through and through.

1. Visualize Kali in the center of your heart, standing on a white lotus. See Kali carried outside your body on your breath, taking her leave through the left nostril. She then is positioned in space facing the meditator.
2. Kali assumes the form of a wild, naked adolescent, of great beauty; her skin is midnight blue, almost black. Her wild hair descends to mid-thigh. Her chest points into the darkness. Her yoni is visible—open to the universe.

3. Visualize Kali wearing a skirt made of severed arms, with a collar of fifty dead men's heads. Her dark skin is smeared with blood. She sticks out her long, long tongue. Her three eyes give her smiling face a radiant look that is overflowing with pleasure and love. She is wearing a gold ring in her right nostril as well as two earrings. Her power is terrifying for ordinary mortals, delicious for heroes.

4. Kali has four arms. In the upper right hand she brandishes a cleaver; in the lower right hand she holds a trident. In the upper left hand she brandishes the head of the ego, freshly severed, the blood and substance of which she collects in a bowl made from the top of a skull that she holds in her lower left hand.

5. Kali utters a terrifying cry, which Mahakala, the Lord of Time, sends her from the depths. Blood flows from her mouth. She is mounted on her tiger and is surrounded by jackals who are her companions in graveyards and cremation fields.

❖ Kali's Temple Is the Meditator's Body

This practice demonstrates that no external temple is needed for the devotee to worship Kali. The meditator's own body becomes the sacred space. This practice employs the use of *mudras*. A *mudra* is a symbolic or ritual gesture that can involve the entire body but is most often done with the hands. In this practice the various mudras and mantras are expressions of devotion and the aspiration to become one with the Goddess. In the first section, the thumb is touched to each of the fingers of the hand in turn, each representing a symbolic bow or petition to the Goddess.

❖ Bowing to the Goddess

1. Kali, on her lotus, is brought to the center of the heart, through the right nostril, as you chant:

OM
KRIM KRIM KRIM
HUM HUM
HRIM HRIM
Daksine
Kalike
KRIM KRIM KRIM
HUM HUM
HRIM HRIM
svaha!

You who transform the subtle body
to infinite perfection,
cut away the ego!
O Goddess
who banishes all darkness,
cut away the ego!
All I do is merge with you!

OM KRIM kalyai namah!

I pay homage to the Goddess Kali who banishes
darkness!

2. Touching thumb to index finger, chant:

OM KRAM angusthabhyam namah!

OM KRAM, I bow with my thumb!

3. Touching thumb to index finger, chant:

   OM KRIM tarjanibhyam svaha!

   OM KRIM, with my index finger all I do is merge with the
   Goddess!

4. Touching thumb to middle finger, chant:

   OM KRUM madhyamabhyam vasat!

   OM KRUM, with my middle finger, purify!

5. Touching thumb to ring finger, chant:

   OM KRAIM anamikabhyam hum!

   OM KRAIM, with my ring finger, cut away the ego!

6. Touching thumb to little finger, chant:

   OM KRAIM kanisthikabhyam vausat!

   OM KRAIM, with the little finger, ultimate purity!

7. Chant the following mantra and turn the hands facing forward while saying *karatal kar;* turn them facing backward
   while saying *prsthabhyam;* and clap the hands together
   while saying *phat.*

   OM krah karatakal kar prsthabhyam astraya phat!

   OM, I bow before the Goddess Kali armed with my
       courage!

   OM KRIM kalyai namah!

   OM KRIM, I bow before the Goddess Kali who banishes
       darkness!

◈ Purifying the Body

In this section the thumb is used to form what is known as the *tattva mudra* (see fig. 5.1), in which it touches the first phalanx of the ring finger, then the hand touches specific parts of the body while particular mantras are chanted.

1. With the right hand taking the tattva mudra, touch the center of the heart and chant:

   OM KRAM hrdayaya namah!

   OM KRAM, I bow in my heart!

2. With the right hand taking the tattva mudra, touch the top of the head and chant:

   OM KRIM sirase svaha!

   OM KRIM, at the top of the head I merge with the Goddess!

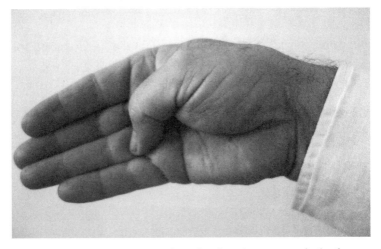

Fig. 5.1. In the tattva mudra, the thumb must touch the first phalanx of the ring finger.

3. With the right hand taking the tattva mudra, touch the back of the head and chant:

   OM KRUM sikhayai vasat!

   OM KRUM, at the back of the head, purify!

4. With the two hands taking the tattva mudra, cross the arms and chant:

   OM KRAIM kavachaya hum!

   OM KRAIM, crossing the arms, cut away ego!

5. With the right hand taking the tattva mudra, touch the three eyes at the same time with the index finger, middle finger, and ring finger and chant:

   OM KRAUM netratrayaya vausat!

   OM KRAUM, with the three eyes, ultimate purity!

6. Chant the following mantra and turn the hands facing forward while saying *karatal kar;* turn them facing backward while saying *prsthabhyam;* and clap the hands together while saying *phat.*

   OM krah karatakal kar prsthabhyam astraya phat!

   OM I bow before the Goddess Kali armed with my
      courage!

   OM KRIM kalyai namah!

   OM KRIM, I bow before the Goddess Kali who banishes
      darkness!

7. With the right hand taking the tattva mudra, touch the head and chant:

OM namah

8. With the right hand taking the tattva mudra, touch the sexual organ and chant:

STRIM namah

9. With the right hand taking the tattva mudra, touch the anus and chant:

EM namah

10. With the right hand taking the tattva mudra, touch the navel and chant:

STRIM namah

11. With the right hand taking the tattva mudra, touch the heart and chant:

AIM namah

12. With the right hand taking the tattva mudra, touch the throat and chant:

KLIM namah

13. With the right hand taking the tattva mudra, touch the third eye and chant:

SAIM namah

14. With the right hand taking the tattva mudra, touch the right shoulder and chant:

   OM namah

15. With the right hand taking the tattva mudra, touch the left shoulder and chant:

   SRIM namah

16. With the right hand taking the tattva mudra, touch the right foot and chant:

   HRIM namah

17. With the right hand taking the tattva mudra, touch the left foot and chant:

   KLIM namah

18. Repeat this mantra 108 times:

   OM KRIM kalyai namah!

   OM KRIM, I bow before the Goddess Kali who banishes darkness!

THE KALI YANTRA

The contemplation of Kali can also take the form of meditation on her *yantra*. The word *yantra* in Sanskrit literally means "a support or instrument." A yantra is "a mystic diagram used as a symbol of the Divine as well as of its powers and aspects."[1] In the Kali yantra the five triangles and their

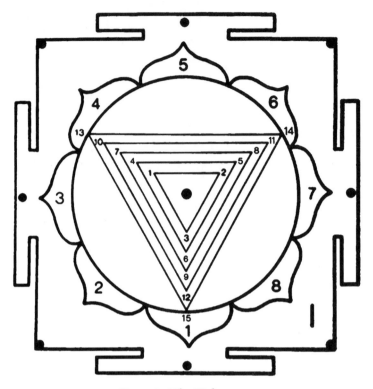

Fig. 5.2. The Kali yantra

fifteen points represent the fifteen Kali Nityas, the fifteen days of the black moon. The eight-petalled lotus represents the eight chakras of the Matsyendranath system in which the eight Bhairava and the eight Bhairavi, the subtle, secret nocturnal aspects of Shiva, manifest and join together. The triangle represents the yoni, the source of the cosmos, power, and creation, the Cosmic Mother. The central point represents the center of the cosmos, the infinite. The Kali yantra should be projected into dark blue space in front of the face; it can be small or as large as the body of the practitioner.

THE RITUAL OF KALI AND SACRED UNION

The instructions given here for the ritual of the Sacred Union generally follow the suggestions given in the *Nirrutara Tantra*. If the ritual of Kali will include sexual celebration, it is preceded by rituals to make the body sacred, including locating the planets; the fifty pithas, or sacred sites; and the eight chakras on the body.

✥ Ritual of Making the Shiva/Shakti Body Sacred

Before the bodies of the *kaulikas* (the practitioners, the Kali worshippers) are made sacred, the site itself is prepared. Then the practitioners are ritually located in that space for initiation.

1. Purify the site by shouting three times *KLIM PATH!*
2. Draw a mandala with vermillion, sandalwood, or water facing the altar where Kali, Queen of Kaula, is located.
   a. First draw a square beginning in the upper right corner.
   b. Then draw a triangle in the square, with the point facing the altar.
3. Position yourself in the center of the triangle with the point facing forward.
4. Call upon the guru by his name, "Kaula."
5. Call upon the lineage.
6. Call upon the red yoginis of the great practice (see chapter 6).
7. Enter into the nondual state of spontaneous meditation, facing the kaulika who is going to be initiated. Whisper in her (or his) ear her (or his) initiation name, which should include one of the 100 names of Kali or of Tripura, followed

by "Anandabhairavi" (for a woman) or "Anandabhairava" (for a man).

❖ Placing the Planets

With the hand in tattva mudra, touch the various parts of the body to link them to the Goddess, who takes the form of all the planets.

AIM HRIM SHRIM AM AM IM IM: Aries (right foot)

AIM HRIM SHRIM UM UM: Taurus (right of sexual organ)

AIM HRIM SHRIM RM RM LM LM: Gemini (right belly)

AIM HRIM SHRIM EM AIM: Cancer (right of the heart)

AIM HRIM SHRIM OM AUM: Leo (right shoulder)

AIM HRIM SHRIM AM AH SHHM SHAM HAM LAM:
   Virgo (right head)

AIM HRIM SHRIM KAM KAHM GAM GHAM NAM:
   Libra (left head)

AIM HRIM SHRIM CHAM CCHAM JAM JHAM NAM:
   Scorpio (left shoulder)

AIM HRIM SHRIM TAM THAM DAM DHAM:
   Sagittarius (left of the heart)

AIM HRIM SHRIM TAM THAM DAM DHAN:
   Capricorn (left belly)

AIM HRIM SHRIM PAM PHAM BAN BHAM MAM:
   Aquarius (left of sexual organ)

AIM HRIM SHRIM YAM RAM LAM VAM KSHAM:
   Pisces (left foot)

❖ Locating the Pithas on the Body

In this practice the body is made sacred by placing upon it the sacred sites (pithas) corresponding to the locations where the dismembered parts of the body of Shakti fell to earth.

As you chant the mantra, touch each location on the body (once again with your hand in tattva mudra) to associate it with the sacred site.

AIM HRIM SHRIM AM Kamarupa: head

AIM HRIM SHRIM AM Varanasi: face

AIM HRIM SHRIM IM Nepal: right eye

AIM HRIM SHRIM IM Paudrardhana: left eye

AIM HRIM SHRIM UM Purasthira Kashmir: right ear

AIM HRIM SHRIM UM Kanyakubja: left ear

AIM HRIM SHRIM RM Purnasheila: right nostril

AIM HRIM SHRIM RM Arbudachala: left nostril

AIM HRIM SHRIM RM Amritakheshvara: right cheek

AIM HRIM SHRIM LM Ekamraya: left cheek

AIM HRIM SHRIM EM Trisrotasi: upper lip

AIM HRIM SHRIM AIM Kamakoli: lower lip

AIM HRIM SHRIM OM Kailash: upper teeth

AIM HRIM SHRIM AUM Brigunagara: lower teeth

AIM HRIM SHRIM AM Khedara: tip of the tongue

AIM HRIM SHRIM AH Chandra Pushkar: throat

AIM HRIM SHRIM KAM Shirupa: right shoulder joint

AIM HRIM SHRIM KHAM Omkhara: right shoulder

AIM HRIM SHRIM GAM Jalandhara: right wrist

AIM HRIM SHRIM GHAM Himalaya: base of the right fingers

AIM HRIM SHRIM NAM Kulanthaka: tips of right fingers

AIM HRIM SHRIM CHAM Devikota: left shoulder joint

AIM HRIM SHRIM CCHAM Gokarna: left shoulder

AIM HRIM SHRIM JAM Maruteshvara: left wrist

AIM HRIM SHRIM JHAM Attahasa: base of left fingers

AIM HRIM SHRIM NAM Viraja: tips of left fingers

AIM HRIM SHRIM TAM Rajageha: right leg joint

AIM HRIM SHRIM THAM Mahapatha: right knee

AIM HRIM SHRIM DAM Kolapura: right ankle

AIM HRIM SHRIM DHAM Elapura: sole of right foot

AIM HRIM SHRIM NAM Kolesvara: toes of right foot

AIM HRIM SHRIM TAM Jayantika: left leg joint

AIM HRIM SHRIM THAM Ujayini: left knee

AIM HRIM SHRIM DAM Chitra: left ankle

AIM HRIM SHRIM DHAM Kshirika: sole of left foot

AIM HRIM SHRIM NAM Hastinapura: toes of left foot

AIM HRIM SHRIM PAM Udisha: right side

AIM HRIM SHRIM PHAM Prayag: left side

AIM HRIM SHRIM BAM Shathisha: back

AIM HRIM SHRIM BHAM Mayapuri: navel

AIM HRIM SHRIM MAM Jalesha: belly

AIM HRIM SHRIM YAM Malaya: heart

AIM HRIM SHRIM RAM Shri Shaila: right shoulder

AIM HRIM SHRIM LAM Meru: nape of the neck

AIM HRIM SHRIM VAM Girivara: left shoulder

AIM HRIM SHRIM SHAM Mahendra:

heart to the center of the right palm

AIM HRIM SHRIM SHAM Vamana:

heart to the center of the left palm

AIM HRIM SHRIM SAM Hiranyapura:

heart to the center of the sole of the right foot

AIM HRIM SHRIM HAM Mahalashmipura:

heart to the center of the sole of the left foot

AIM HRIM SHRIM LAM Oddyhana:

heart to the sexual area

AIM HRIM SHRIM KSHAM Chayachatra:

heart to the top of the head

❖ *Locating the Eight Chakras*

This exercise is designed to help you locate the eight chakras in your body. With your hand in tattva mudra, you will touch each part of the body named below to locate the eight chakras, while simultaneously chanting the Sanskrit letter associated with each corresponding chakra. You will notice that—in typical tantric reversal—the chakras in this exercise are numbered from top to bottom, as opposed to the more conventional numbering from bottom to top. This follows the practice described by Matsyendranath in his Tantra.

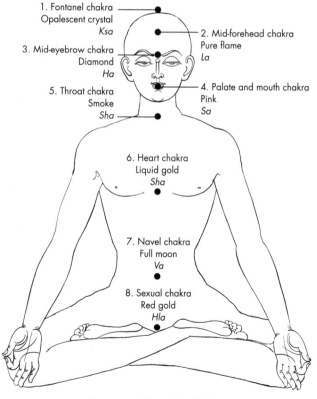

1. Fontanel chakra
Opalescent crystal
Ksa

2. Mid-forehead chakra
Pure flame
La

3. Mid-eyebrow chakra
Diamond
Ha

4. Palate and mouth chakra
Pink
Sa

5. Throat chakra
Smoke
Sha

6. Heart chakra
Liquid gold
Sha

7. Navel chakra
Full moon
Va

8. Sexual chakra
Red gold
Hla

Fig. 5.3. The eight chakras

1. Touch the fontanel at the crown of your head while chanting *Ksa*.
2. Touch the middle of your forehead while chanting *La*.
3. Touch between your eyebrows while chanting *Ha*.
4. Touch your mouth while chanting *Sa*.
5. Touch the base of your throat while chanting *Sha* ("sh" pronounced as in *shun*).
6. Touch the heart center between your breasts while chanting *Sha* ("s" pronounced as in *sure*).
7. Touch your navel while chanting *Va*.
8. Touch the sexual center at your perineum while chanting *Hla*.

❖ Ritual of Sacred Union

If the ritual of Kali includes sexual celebration, the two initiates having become Shiva/Kali, they then proceed to the sacred Kaula union of the Bhairava chakra, in which they are joined heart to heart. Because the sexual organs are considered to be heart centers too, the initiates may also be joined in physical sexual union. The partners can be *pujya* (object of worship) or *bhogya* (partner of sexual worship). The ritual is the same, followed by a visualization of union for the former and an actual sexual union for the latter. In both cases the sacred union may be considered valid only during the ceremony of the Sacred Circle, in which the sacred ritual is practiced in a group of yogis and yoginis, or for a longer period.

According to Matsyendranath, this movement of worship includes all beings without distinction. The women can be yoginis, partners, disciples, or untouchables. There is no restriction in the Kaula path, because every woman is the Goddess just as every man is Shiva.

Once the ritual has been experienced, Shiva/Kali unite freely so long as they are in a nondual state. Kali's body becomes the whole collection of sacred sites, and the kaulika who immerses himself/herself in that simultaneously enters these locations. The *amrta* (ambrosia) of the kaulikas is the sublime essence of Shakti consumed at the source. Amrta is also lunar essence visualized in the secret chakra. It bathes the yogi with lunar milk in the yoga of Matsyendranath.

1. Chanting the appropriate mantra 108 times, the two kaulikas meditate, respectively, on Anandabhairava for the female initiate and on Anandabhairavi for the male initiate, full of life and youthfulness, luminous, their faces radiant as the full moon and who are in amorous union floating in midnight blue space, blending their essences in continuous quivering.

   OM anandabhairavaya namah!
   OM anandabhairaviyai namah!

2. Bless the wine with the following mantra chanted in unison three times.

   AM HRIM KROM svaha!

3. They drink wine to consecrate the Sacred Union.*
4. In the culmination of the Kaula ritual, Shiva and Kali are united through the visualized or real amorous union, accompanied by the following mantras, beginning with

---

*The participants drink a fermented beverage from sources such as palm, wheat, or barley mixed with honey, not grape wine.

the Tripura mantra, which seals the sacred union, chanted three times:

AIM KLIM SAUH tripurayai namah!

May this Shakti (Shiva) be mine.

May this Shakti (Shiva) be pure.

May she (he) be mine!

HRIM devesi

May her yoni (his lingam) emit streams of
        sublime essence!

SAUH

In her yoni (his lingam).

*OM AIM KLIM SAUH SHRIM HRIM PATH
        svaha!*
OM HSAUM VIM VIM VIM VIM

Oh! Woman of knowledge!

Oh! Lunar milk!

Come! Come profusely!

THE RETREAT INTO ABSOLUTE DARKNESS

Ideally, the ritual of Kali is to be practiced as a retreat that takes place in complete darkness. Few centers offer this possibility, but if you wish to offer this option to practitioners, you can improvise by finding an isolated location. Light can be kept out with black plastic tarps covering the windows. Given the difficulties inherent in being in darkness and to avoid comings and goings, it is essential that each room have a bathroom so that its air circulation will ventilate the room as well. The corridor leading to the room should also be without light so that you can enter the room to bring food to the practitioners.

It is essential as well that the person who is conducting the retreat be nearby, listening, and able to enter the room at any moment, because anxiety attacks can happen. This type of retreat can only be done with a few individuals who are well experienced in the path. It is totally inappropriate for those whose personality is delicate or disturbed.

Comfort is important, and the quality of the food as well.

The initial days are spent simply confronting the darkness with no other practice than silent sitting. It will not be long before there will occur what Rimbaud called "the great unhinging of all the senses" in which sense perceptions leave their accustomed territory. This confusion will assist in the emergence of all those things that have been hidden or repressed; the practitioners will observe the appearance and release of powerful emotions in this theater of the unconscious.

At first the fear of confronting one's own darkness will encourage the practitioners to sleep a lot—so much so that after two or three days they hardly sleep at all. This is the point at which the confrontation with darkness really begins.

For individuals to let go completely, the physical presence of the master, actively listening, is very important. Once the mind begins to calm, the participants can then begin the preliminary practices, followed by the Kali ritual. The practice will release a new wave of letting go. The darkness makes time disappear. It slips away from us, and we become Kali.

6

Advancing on the Kaula Path

Meditation on the Eight Chakras, the Yoginis' Ultimate Practice of the Heart, and the Devouring of Inner Demons

*I*n the Kaula school the yoga practices and the visualizations activate the eight chakras, each of which is composed of eight petals. They are linked to the practice of the eight Sahaja Mothers, or Red Goddesses. Each Mother is visualized as sitting on one of the petals.

> Brahmi, situated in the petal above the lotus, symbolizes *buddhi*—pure intelligence.
> Mahesvari, in the petal below to the left (in the counterclockwise direction), symbolizes the creation place of the "I."
> Kumari, in the next petal, symbolizes capricious, fluctuating thought.

Vaisnavi, in the next petal, symbolizes listening, the voice, melodious sounds.

Varahi, in the next petal, symbolizes touch, the skin.

Indrani, or Vajrahasta, in the next petal, symbolizes seeing, form.

Chamunda, in the next petal, symbolizes taste, the tongue.

Aghoresi, in the last petal, symbolizes the sense of smell, the nose.

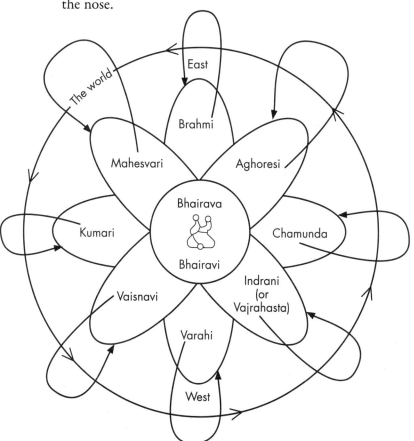

Fig. 6.1. The eight Sahaja Mothers on the eight petals

The heart of the mandala is associated with our heart, from which the highest consciousness springs forth. It is the foundation of all that exists and vibrates: body, thought, breath, energy, knowledge. It is the center of the sense organs and center of the divinities. Through our senses and our mind the eight goddesses continually send forth their unparalleled harvest toward the heart. "The goddesses of the organs of sensing shine on the throne of your body. They are identical to the cosmos and in their midst the supreme Bhairava/Bhairavi are resplendent," says Gorakshanath.

All the faculties are thus in uninterrupted exchange with the center of the mandala where Bhairavi and Bhairava are intertwined. All the energy goes toward the center while the energy of Bhairavi and Bhairava—which incarnates the secret, the night, deep contemplation—returns toward us like a divine nectar.

Matsyendranath in his *Kaulajnananirnaya Tantra* describes the eight chakras and the powers that are connected to each one of them. He speaks of the Mothers: "The Sahaja Mothers are very powerful and very terrifying. They are beautiful and colored red. They even allow a *pashu* [an animal-natured or limited being] to reach the heavenly state. They give birth to living beings and they are at the origin of the genesis of the being inside the womb. . . . The Siddhas, all beings worship the eight Mothers."[1]

This configuration is found in each of the eight chakras. Matsyendranath continues: "All that was formed by combinations and in the same way all yoginis should be thought of as able to connect in this way. Multiplying eight times eight you get the sixty-four yoginis. This is in accordance with the order which has been assigned to them."[2]

The eight Mothers give birth to the sixty-four yoginis:

Jaya	Virabadra	Bhuvaneswari
Vijaya	Doomangi	Chataki
Jayanthi	Kalakapriya	Mahamari
Aparajitha	Korarakthakshi	Yamaduthi
Divya Yogini	Viswarupa	Karalini
Maha Yogini	Abhayankari	Kesini
Sidha Yogini	Virakowmari	Marthini
Ganeshwara	Chandika	Romajanga
Yogini	Varahi	Nivarini
Predasini	Mundadarini	Visalini
Dakini	Rakshasi	Kaarmuki
Kamala	Bhairavi	Loli
Kaalaratri	Dwangshini	Adomuki
Nisasari	Doomrangi	Mundakradarini
Dankarini	Predavahini	Vyakrini
Roudri	Katwangi	Kangkshini
Hoomkarini	Dirgalamboshti	Predarupini
Urdvakesini	Maalini	Durjati
Virupakshi	Matthayogini	Kori
Suklangi	Kalini	Karali
Narabhojini	Chakrini	Vishalambini
Patkari	Kangali	

Matsyendranath asserts: "It is only in knowing these sixty-four periods that they bestow the siddhis, and not otherwise. The secret order of the sixty-four yoginis has thus been uttered by me and in the clearest terms. You ought to remember it with devotion."[3]

In India there are still some circular temples devoted to Kaula rites. Bhairava and Bhairavi are at the center in amorous union, surrounded by sixty-four niches, each of which shelters a Red Mother. One of the best-preserved temples is located in Orissa at Ranipur-Jharial.

Chakra 1: The fontanel chakra, the color of opalescent crystal, corresponds to the Sanskrit letter *Ksa*.

"The first chakra bestows the power to unite with the yoginis, the power to make oneself small, and . . . effective achievement in meditation and sadhana."

Chakra 2: The chakra in the middle of the forehead, the color of pure flame, corresponds to the Sanskrit letter *La*.

"With . . . meditation . . . on the second chakra, you gain the power to mesmerize all beings, the ability to break or project objects at a distance and the ability to subjugate others."

Chakra 3: The chakra between the eyebrows, the color of diamond, corresponds to the Sanskrit letter *Ha*.

"Whoever practices frequently the method of the third great chakra can subtly slip into someone else's body; in addition, he is able to see the future."

Chakra 4: The chakra of the palate and the mouth, pink in color, corresponds to the Sanskrit letter *Sa*.

"The fourth chakra is the . . . provider of powers of calming, liberation, and voluptuousness. If you venerate this chakra. . . , you become capable of instantaneously paralyzing another person. . . , you attain the power of invisibility and the power of listening to conversations."

Chakra 5: The chakra at the base of the throat, the color of smoke, corresponds to the Sanskrit letter *Sa*.

"By meditating . . . on the fifth great chakra, you are able to express yourself like a *rsi*, to move about like the wind, and to bring someone's conversation to a halt."

Chakra 6: The chakra of the heart, the color of liquid gold, corresponds to the Sanskrit letter *Sa*.

"The sixth chakra bestows teaching, power, and freedom."

Chakra 7: The chakra of the navel, the color of the full moon, corresponds to the Sanskrit letter *Va*.

"Whoever . . . conducts his sadhana on the seventh chakra . . . obtains the power to enslave others. He displays the ability to paralyze, to subjugate others, and to free himself from the chains of *samsara*."

Chakra 8: The perineal, or sexual, chakra, the color of red gold, corresponds to the Sanskrit letter *Hla*.

"The eighth chakra . . . allows anyone to cause death and to travel far away. Also it bestows the power to generate paralysis and illusion in others. He who resides in the great chakra is the beloved of the yoginis."

The quotations from Matsyendranath shown in figure 6.2 demonstrate that the magic context appears clearly in his teachings. In the eighth century the power to subjugate, paralyze, and kill were part of the yogi's armory. When these teachings were transmitted to Kashmir, Abhinavagupta and the other masters paid no attention to these powers and adopted the mystical experience stripped of this antique context.

✧ Meditation to Set the Eight Chakras in Motion

To render homage and set the wheels (chakras) in motion, Matsyendranath provides the following practice.

"You should always meditate on the eight chakras using a beautiful and intense luminous flame that you move eight times through each of the centers. Through your own will you become the Lord of Breath which is capable of causing enthusiasm by being unified with Kancuki Devi herself."[4]

THE YOGINIS' PRACTICE OF THE HEART

As numerous Tantras make known, the heart is the main energy center in the Kaula path. The Yoginis' Practice of the Heart is considered to be the ultimate practice, because it continually connects the sadhana to the energy of the heart. It does this by taking the world perceived in its reality and creating a vortex that ceaselessly feeds the energy of the heart. Reality

Fig. 6.2 (opposite). The eight chakras. The quotations appearing to the right of each chakra are from Matsyendranath's Kaulajnananirnaya Tantra, *translated from Sanskrit [into French] by Dominique Boubouleix.*

and the Absolute then merge. This is the secret practice of the sixty-four yoginis that sets the eight chakras vibrating. It is the summit of a path leading to the incomparable and the discovery of the limitless. "The heart is the Goddess," says Abhinavagupta.

The heart is also called Shaktichakra. The energy of the heart turns around and around endlessly, forming a double spiral: the Red Goddesses emerge from the center, harvest the Real, and conduct the intimate substance back into the heart of the practitioner. The heart is like a beehive, and the Red Goddesses are like bees that extract pollen from the flowers and carry it back to nourish the queen of the heart. This continuous pouring forth leads to blessedness and continuous vibration (spanda). It dissolves knots in the ego and brings deliverance.

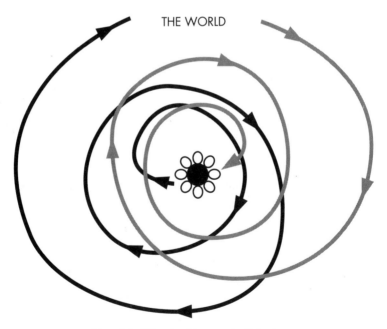

THE WORLD

Fig. 6.3. The double spiral of the heart

Abhinavagupta points out that the pleasures of the senses linked to the ego deplete the reservoir of the heart while the Yoginis' Practice of the Heart fills it ceaselessly. This practice leads to the constant integration of the Real into the center of the heart. It is through this practice received from Sambunatha, master of the Kaula tradition, that the awakening of Abhinavagupta took place. This practice leads to the ultimate.

There are, however, three obstacles to overcome.

1. The obstacle of egoistic individuality
2. The obstacle of not recognizing one's plenitude and one's identity with the Divine
3. The obstacle that renders pleasures of the senses a distraction and a loss of absolute essence

Attachment is an identification with the physical body; freedom is an identification with the cosmic body. Abhinavagupta says that he who at every moment dissolves the universe in his own consciousness and then manifests it once again by projecting it toward the world becomes Bhairava/Bhairavi.

As this is the supreme practice of the Kaula path, it is accessible only through direct transmission after all other sadhanas have been completed successfully.

Some things to keep in mind regarding this practice:

• Become aware that reality is identical to your own heart—the place where the Red Goddesses reside.
• Levels of reality are layered around absolute consciousness.

- The fire of the knower-subject, the experience under the aspect of the sun, and the moon of the known-object form a spiral that pours into the heart and emerges from it endlessly.
- Reality dissolves in the fire of the heart; reality springs forth from the heart.
- This ceaseless vortex reveals the true nature of the Self.
- The Shaktichakra of the heart delights in all sensorial, emotional, and mental forms, and the Red Goddesses ceaselessly harvest reality in order to dissolve it in the heart.
- External objects are recognized as identical to absolute consciousness in the fire of nonduality.
- The footprints and residues of perceptions dissolve.
- This is the union of Bhairava/Bhairavi in the heart.
- Through this practice you attain supernatural powers, which match the Real perfectly.

✦ Kali Practice: The Devouring of Inner Demons

Here "demons" are not to be understood as external menacing entities; you need to realize—as did the great yogini Machig—that "all demons are manifestations of the ego."

1. In a relaxed and comfortable posture, realize that all demons are forms springing forth from ego.
2. Consider the twelve categories of demons and choose which one you want to work on.
   1. Lack
   2. Fear
   3. Abandonment
   4. Neurotic love

     5. Addiction

     6. Pride, positive or negative judgment of oneself or others

     7. Family, father, mother

     8. Anger, violence

     9. Shame, guilt, unworthiness

    10. Vanity

    11. Cruelty

    12. Sadness, depression

3. Travel through your body looking to meet the chosen demon. What is his usual abode or room (such as an organ, group of muscles, bone, or joint)? Is this an itinerant demon, or does he always hide in the same spot?

4. Once you have found the demon's abode, enter that room with all your senses on the alert. At first the room will be fairly dark. Sit down and scrutinize the dark. What do you feel, what do you see? Does the demon have objects around him? Protective animals perhaps? Does he himself appear? What shape does he adopt?

5. How many arms, legs, eyes? What does he smell like? What color is he? Do you see flames, animal idols?

6. Feel the demon's frustration in not being able to be in full possession of you. Feel that your resistance gives him strength and ensures that you must struggle. This is the first time you have faced the demon, the first time you have seen him. No longer is this some abstract entity. And to appease him you are going to offer him your body, your essence. He can devour you, drink you, absorb you.

7. When the demon is satisfied, the tension disappears. Face him without fear for the first time. Your resistance gave

the demon his charge, his strength. Imagine a little golden sphere in the center of your heart. Perhaps your confrontation surprised him, drove him crazy, made him violent; maybe he is brandishing weapons, belching terrible sounds. But stay in the presence of the golden sphere, in the calm of peaceful breathing.

8. As you stay in the room, visualize that your body is floating in midnight blue space and that in this space, all around you, dozens of Kalis appear forming an unassailable sphere. Armed with their cleavers and their tridents, they excitedly await the battle.

9. Look the demon in the eyes, even if they are bloody, black, or terrifying. After breathing in deeply, feel that in the sudden powerful breathing out the golden sphere expands, explodes, moves out of your body and hurls the demon out of his room, through your body and then into space where the famished Kalis are waiting for him. They descend on him, cut him to pieces, and devour him.

10. As soon as the demon has disappeared, the golden sphere returns to the room and surrounds it like a halo with gold that is half liquid, half vapor. You float in the golden light and thank the Goddess.

This practice is intense and tiring. Only deal with one demon at a time. No more than one each day. After the practice, take a shower or dive into a river, a lake, or the sea.

It is possible that certain demons will make a new attempt and try to take back their space in the body. In this case, repeat the practice with this demon before taking on other demons.

Later on, since the strength of the demon has been lessened, do an on-the-spot practice: as soon as you feel him in his room, expel him directly with the golden sphere. Don't let him reinstall himself.

This practice makes it possible to remove the five coverings or limitations of maya (kancukas) by seeing how they are linked to the following five absolute qualities.

- Omnipotence, linked to limited action
- Omniscience, linked to limitation of knowledge
- Completeness, linked to incompleteness
- Eternity, linked to the perception of time that limits us
- The complete freedom of the Self, linked to limiting submission

7

Hymns and Songs in Praise of Kali

ABHINAVAGUPTA'S HYMN IN PRAISE OF THE TWELVE KALIS

Abhinavagupta wrote a hymn of praise to the twelve Kalis, which gives an overview of the highest mystical path followed by the worshipper of Kali in all stages of the spiritual experience. Following is how he describes the passage and the experience of the various Kalis that lead to the Absolute.

> The first, Shristikali, creation of objects, is the Supreme Consciousness [Parasamvit] when the will to create arises in her, and the would-be creation shines in outline objectively within her.

> The second, Raktakali, or experience of objects, is when, after the manifestation of the objective world, the Supreme Consciousness manifests herself as the means of

knowledge [the five senses] and is affected by the externalized objective world. This is the concept of the power of "preservation" in relation to the object.

The third, Sthitinasakali, termination of the experience of objects, is the Supreme Consciousness intent upon terminating her extrovert form, and, therefore, the objective world, because of her inclination to rest within herself in the form of the consciousness "I have known the object." This is the concept of "annihilation" in relation to the object.

The fourth, Yamakali, doubt about the experience of the object, is the concept of an indefinable power relating to conceptual objects and experience. It leads to the rise of doubt about the objects of experience that is present as a mere idea and to its removal or destruction.

The subtle distinction between the latter two [Sthitinasakali and Yamakali] is, "I have known the object" and "the objects of experience are non-different from me."

The fifth, Samharakali, or dissociation of objects from external norms, centres round the power of destruction. After the destruction of doubt, or its objects, the Supreme Consciousness brings about the disappearance of the externality of the objects and groups them within, as one with herself.

The sixth, Mrtyukali, total merging of object in subject, is of the nature of death [*Mrtyu*], causing the disappearance of the externality of objects. But it is related to objectivity, in so far as it realizes objectivity as non-different from itself. But this objectivity can have being only if it rests on the Subject [*Pramatr*] that is free of all limitations. Mrtyukali is so called because it engulfs even Samharakali.

The seventh, Rudrakali or Bhadrakali, object momentarily reinstated to be finally dissolved, is when, immediately after dissolving the multitude of objects, the Universal Consciousness gives rise to a definite object in the mind of an individual subject. To this object, which is a revived mental picture of a particular action done in the past, doubt is related. The doubt about it is, whether it was right or wrong. And the certainty about it being right or wrong is responsible for its fruition in the pleasant or unpleasant experiences here and hereafter.

The eighth, Martandakali, merging of the twelve faculties, is Universal Consciousness in that she brings about the merging of all the twelve means of knowledge, the *Indriyas*—which are the five senses of perception, the five organs of action, *Manas* [Mind], and *Buddhi* [Intellect]— in the *Ahamkara* or ego-consciousness. Martandakali represents *Anakhya* [indefinable] power in relation to the means of knowledge, in so far as it brings about the identification of the twelve means of knowledge with the ego-consciousness, to the extent that they completely lose their being, and become unnameable.

The preceding four Kalis are the aspects of the Universal

Consciousness which destroy the means of knowledge and action. The following four, beginning with Paramarkakali, are such as destroy the limited subject.

The ninth, Paramarkakali, is merging of ego-consciousness into the limited subject of "spirit." It represents the particular power in relation to the limited subject in so far as it brings about the emergence of the limited subject through merging in it of *Ahamkara,* ego-consiousness.

The tenth, Kalanalarudrakali, merging Spirit with Pure Wisdom, is the particular power of the Universal Consciousness when she brings about the merging of a limited self with the Universal Self, in whom all objectivity has its being. This power of the limited subject resting in the Universal is experienced as "I am all this." Because of her capacity for holding everything, even time, within herself, she is called Mahakali, the Supreme Kali.

The experience which characterizes Mahakala [Time transcending time] is, "I am all this." But there is a yet higher experience, in which the "this" element is absent. The distinction between these two experiences is that in the former the "I" rests on the "this," but in the latter, the "this" being absent, the "I" rests within itself.

The eleventh, Mahakalakali, merging Pure Wisdom in Energy, is the Universal Consciousness as she brings about the merging of the "I"—which shines in opposition to "this," as "I am all this," into the "Pure I," the "Perfect

I," the "Akula," which is free of all relations to "objectivity," to "this." Subject is annihilated here.

The twelfth, Mahabhairavacandograghorakali, merging Energy in the Absolute, embraces "Perfect I," "Akula," subject, object, the means of knowledge as well as knowledge in perfect unity with Pure Consciousness.

The stage is called "Para." It does not manifest itself in subject, object, the means of knowledge or knowledge, and therefore is free from all relations. It is "total."[1]

THE HUNDRED NAMES OF KALI

This hymn is an extract from the *Mahanirvana Tantra*.[2]

> *HRIM,* O fearsome one!
> *SHRIM,* O kindly one!
> *KRIM,* you who destroy Time!
> Origin of all manifestation,
> Womb of Shaktis,
> Destroyer of the illusions of our Kali Yuga,
> Salve for the ascetics of Shiva,
> Devourer of Shiva-Rudra who devours,
> Rhythm of Time,
> Bursting forth of the play of final dissolution,
> Spouse of he who carries the lunar crescent,
> Container of the limitless,

Ocean of the nectar of compassion,

Who shares in the suffering of your creatures,

Source of all mercy,

Infinite understanding,

Accessible through your grace alone,

You, Fire,

Cat-like,

She of the black skin,

Pleasure of the lord of creation,

Dusky night,

You, Desire,

You, however, who release the shackles of desire,

Dark as a storm cloud,

Adorned with the crescent moon,

You tear away the veil of ignorance woven by the Kali
    Yuga,

Kaumari, Virgin who takes pleasure in her creation
    without being possessed,

Refuge of those who conduct rituals to honor virgins,

Rejoicing in the festivals held in honor of virgins,

Gauri, the nubile virgin,

You wander in the infinity of your creation as in a
    forest of Kadamba,

The flowers of the forest of Kadamba delight you,

The high timberland of the forest of Kadamba
    encircles your domain,

Flower garlands from Kadamba adorn your neck,

You, youth itself,

You have the soft and husky voice of he who swallowed
    poison to release ambrosia,

The sound of your voice evokes the passionate duet of
    the *chakravaka* birds that the waters separated,

You drink mead,

You rejoice in the offering of mead,

A human skull is your cup,

You wear a collar made up of bones,

Lotuses delight you,

You are seated on a lotus,

You dwell at the center of a lotus,

You become drunk from the perfume of the lotus,

You have the swaying gait of a *hamsa* bird,

You liberate from fear,

You take any form you like,

While seated you are enveloped in the form of Desire,

The sphere of Desire is your field of battle,

O splendor,

O vine wrapped around the *kalpa* tree that satisfies all
    desire!

Your beauty is your only adornment,

Adorable incarnation of tenderness,

Gentle body,

Delicate body,

You appreciate the nectar of purified wine from the
    sacrifices,

You favor those who the purified wine refreshes,

You are the very energy of those who worship you drunk
    with this wine,

The worshipping of you using purified wine satisfies
    you,

You immerse yourself in the ocean of purified wine,

You are the protector of whoever conducts ritual
    exercises with this wine,

The perfume of musk thrills you,

The *tilaka* sign drawn on your forehead with musk
    shines forth,

You bless with musk those who worship you,

You are a mother to those who burn musk as incense,

The musk deer is dear to you,

You appreciate eating its musk,

You joyfully breathe the scent of camphor,

You wear garlands of flowers from the camphor tree,

Your body is coated with a paste of camphor and
    sandalwood,

You drink purified wine perfumed with camphor,

You bathe in an ocean of camphor,

You dwell in an ocean of camphor,

You are pleased to be invoked with the seed-syllable
    HUM,

During battle, you ceaselessly emit the terrifying sound
    of the seed-syllable *HUM,*

You, incarnation of tantric path Kaula in which the very
    essence of Shiva/Shakti is worshipped,

Worshipped by the lords of the Kaula path,

Benefactor of the lords of the Kaula path,

Follower of the Kaula path,

You, Joy,

Revealer of the way of the Kaulikas,

Queen of Kashi,

You liberate from the suffering of the triple fire of
    desire,

Blessing of Shiva, King of Kashi,

Pleasure of Shiva, King of Kashi,

Beloved of Shiva, King of Kashi,

When you move, the bells on your belt

And the quivering rings on your toes compose celestial
music,

The middle peak of Mount Sumeru is your radiant
abode,

You are like a ray of sunshine on the golden mountain,

The recitation of the mantra *KLIM*, whose last syllable
expresses the supreme state, delights you,

You are *KLIM*, the seed-syllable of Kama,

You awaken and stimulate the thirst for transcendence,

You remove obstacles from the path of the Kaulikas,

Sovereign of the initiates of the Kaula path,

O you who, with the three seed-syllables *KRIM HRIM
SHRIM*, are freed from the ascendency of death,

I pay homage to you!

HYMN TO KALI

This hymn is part of the *Mahanirvana Tantra*. Most of the
Tantras are anonymous, and their dates are uncertain because
they were transmitted orally before being written down. As
French Indologist and researcher André Padoux stated, "The
history of Tantrism is impossible to write." Most of the Tantras were probably written between the sixth and the tenth
centuries in Kashmir and Nepal.

This hymn to Kali is preceded and followed by the
chanting of Kali's bija mantras.

OM
KRIM KRIM KRIM
HUM HUM
HRIM HRIM
Daksine
Kalike
KRIM KRI, KRIM
HUM HUM
HRIM HRIM
svaha!

Thus shall I praise you, Kali, O Queen of Kasi,
For attaining the object of my desire.
In this hymn I sing praises to your glory,
Wellspring of blessings, O you whom the gods adore.

You are the origin of the world,
You who have no origin;
Hymns, by the hundreds, proclaim this.
Brahma, Vishna, and Shiva themselves cannot know you;
We, however, Mother of Knowing, we worship your
        breasts
Brushed with the golden pollen from the stamens of
        saffron.
O Sovereign of the three bodies, we worship you.
Your perfect form shines with a thousand rising suns;
Your forehead, where three eyes shine, carries the lunar
        crescent;
You hold the trident, the sabre, the severed head of the
        ego, and a cup for collecting the blood.
You are dark as night.

Your eyes, three lotus buds,
Brighten your young face that is a lotus in full bloom;
Voluptuous is your neck adorned with giant pearls formed
     from the severed heads.

O Mother, the ignorant, shot through with doubt and
     hatred,
Cannot conceive of your radiant body,
Highlighted with signs of blood,
Which bends under the weight of your tasty breasts,
O you, accessible solely through the merits
Of an awakened consciousness.

O destroyer of time, O terrifying one, O kindly one!
You are the destroyer of the illusion of the Kali Yuga.

Mother of time, you shine with the fires of the final
     dissolution.
You are fire,
Cat-like, black with dew, dark night,
Liberator of the strictures of limited desire,
Dark as a storm cloud,
You who destroy fear,
Adorable, adorned with great tenderness,
Nourished with sacred ambrosia,
Joyful, you show tantric practitioners the way!

The shades of black are infinite
But your black is wondrous:
If it is contemplated within oneself

It illuminates the lotus of the heart,
Black in form, black in name,
Blacker than darkness,
Whoever contemplates your face is dazed,
It remains unaffected by any other face!

Very sweet is the name of Kali
For he who murmurs it in his heart!

O Wife-Mother of Shiva,
To describe you, wise men have recourse to things
From our physical world.
The holy books evoke you in a subtle form,
Certain call you the Verb,
Others consider you to be the womb of the universe,
But for us, you are, before all things, an ocean of infinite
    love!

Your worshippers visualize you in their hearts.
Your forehead, where your three eyes shine, carries the
    lunar crescent;
You hold the trident, the sabre, the head of the severed
    ego, and a cup for collecting blood.
You are as dark as night.
Your substance is made up of the fifty letters of the
    alphabet
In which the qualities of What Is vibrate.

O Wife of the Conqueror of the three Cities,
You are Shiva united with Parvati,

You are Vishnu embraced by Lakshmi,
You are also Brahma born of the lotus,
You are moreover she who gives forth the Sound
And presides over her formulations
And you are the Energy that animates all that.

I, concentrated on the four sonorous states of
    Kundalini
In which reverberate the moving forces that constitute
    your Name,
May I never lose you, O Divinity Supreme,
Substance and Consciousness of What Is,
You whose throat emits the causal Sound
After Kundalini has pierced the eight chakras.

The Blessed who have triumphed over the six causes of
    error
And have control over their breathing,
Steadfast of spirit, their gaze fixed on the infinite,
These Blessed are contemplating in thought your form
    crowned with the moon,
Your form that shines forth with the burst of the first
    rising sun.

The Tantras proclaim that you created the universe
By assuming the androgynous duality of Shiva/Shakti
And in truth That Is,
O Daughter of the Mountain, Mother of Creation,
For without you
The multitude of worlds would never have been created.

The wives of the lower and higher divinities, together,
Their eyes overflowing with an abundance of ambrosia,
Come to adore you in your den in the golden mountain;
Scattering over you the flowers of celestial trees,
They sing your praises.

I worship in my heart Devi-Kundalini
When she springs up from the *muladhara* chakra, her
    dwelling place,
In order to rise up to Shiva's throne,
Opening one by one the lotuses of the royal path of the
    sushumna;
Her beauty cloaks the flash of lightning
And her body flows with the nectar of Union.

Goddess of three faces,
You who create, maintain, and destroy worlds,
I take refuge at your lotus feet
That are worshipped by Brahma, Vishnu, and Shiva.
You are a land of blessing, a source of Tantras,
Origin of all fullness, your substance is Pure
    Consciousness.

When assuming the face of the moon
You symbolize, O Mother, will and desire
And you create the world vibrating with sounds
With their innumerable effects;
When assuming the solar mask
You have the power to make all things visible
And you maintain creation;

Assuming the aspect of fire you consume the entire
     universe
At the end of time.

Men worship you under multiple names.
Primordial woman: She who rescues from the ocean of
     rebirths;
The Opalescent; the Black One, burned by the fire of yoga,
Goddess of the word and of science;
Shiva/Shakti of the triple gaze,
Who reveals the paths of knowledge,

O Mother of the universe
He who worships you
By singing the verses of this hymn,
Obtains the mastery of words and their power;
He attains you
And the immutable center of the universal gyration of
     worlds.[3]

OM
KRIM KRIM KRIM
HUM HUM
HRIM HRIM
Daksine
Kalike
KRIM KRIM KRIM
HUM HUM
HRIM HRIM
svaha!

In the fire of supreme divinity,
I see you in all manifestation
and I attain union with supreme divinity!

OM santih santih santih!

OM, peace, peace, peace!

SONGS TO KALI

Ramprasad is undoubtedly the most famous of the poets who worshipped Kali. With grace he expresses all her aspects, all her potential. Born in Bengal about 1720, he lived in a hut near the Ganges. Early on he abandoned his job as an accountant. The anecdote of his leaving is beautiful. When he was asked to deliver his account books to his superior, marvelous poems were discovered hastily scribbled in the margins. Instead of reprimanding his employee, his employer provided him with a stipend so that Ramprasad could stop working and spend his days worshipping Kali and writing.

Ramprasad was also the first person to take an initiative to oppose animal sacrifices in the rituals.

Enchantress of hearts
Fresh as a lotus
Her movements are those of a swan.
Tumbling hair is her halo,
Nude, drunk, a cadaver for her seat,
She is expert and undeterred
This child of sixteen.
And beautiful as the full moon!

The rising sun is a moon on her forehead.

Brahma and Vishnu are her set of earrings.

She embodies a thousand charms

And the sweetness of her face

Would even tempt honey!

Beloved of He

Who is carrying the moon in his topknot.

Refuge of Mangala and child of the sun,

Honored by Buddha and Brihaspati,

She has the eyes of a gazelle, the body of a lioness.

She, Destroyer of Evil,

Is worshipped by gods: Hari, Hara, Brahma.

And he takes his place

In the family of the Lord,

He who always worships

The Mother clothed in space.

Very sweet is the name of Kali.

Oh! Sing of it forever!

Imbibe her essence,

And shame on you, my tongue,

Who still wants

Sweets and candy!

At once form and formless,

Kali is the letter K,

Foundation of all that is.

She is pleasure and liberation,

Supreme abode and the one and only Name,

Beyond that what else is there?

In the heart where Kali watches

Run the waters of the Ganges
And when the hour comes
That heart which has become Eternal
Laughs at death!
Light then in yourself the fire of knowledge,
Cast into it the butter of good and evil,
Just as we offer the betel leaf,
Offer your heart, and may your zeal,
Like a sacrificial spoon, foster her worship.
Prasad says: In this way have there been abolished
Divisions in the land of the heart.
My body is the domain of Dakshina Kali.
She has stamped it with her seal.

It is time, O Kali, to come into accord with each
    other.
By taking your measure, O my black Goddess,
I will pierce the mystery of your night.
Your dance Kali, elusive as it is,
How might I grasp it?
On the lotus of my heart I will have her dance
To the music of my soul.
Thus, O my soul, from Kali's footsteps
I will teach you the beat of her rhythm.
I will sacrifice the six rebellious passions.
I will sing Kali's name.
I will meditate on Kali.
Into Kali will I melt,
And this is how my time will take its course.
In all seasons will I follow my path

And Kala, the Great Death, time itself,
With Kali's black, will I smear his face.
Straight at his face, will I throw him Kali!
Prasad says: "O Mother, will I say more?
What more could I express?"
With no complaint, enduring blows,
Never will I forget, never will I abandon Kali.[4]

ᢺ ᢻ

The plenitude of worship takes place in a state of perfect consciousness in which we worship this energy [Kali] everywhere and in which there appears the spontaneous inner vibration that silences the whole universe—the Supreme Heart.

LILIAN SILBURN,
HYMNES AUX KALI

Notes

PREFACE

1. Saraswati, *Shree Maa*.

INTRODUCTION.
KALI AND THE TANTRIC PATH

1. Woodroffe, *Garland of Letters*, 220.
2. Ibid., 220–21.
3. Monier-Williams, *A Sanskrit-English Dictionary*.
4. Wallis, *Tantra Illuminated*, 26.
5. Fischer-Schreiber, Ehrhard, Friedrichs, and Diener, *The Encyclopedia of Eastern Philosophy and Religion*, 354.

CHAPTER 1.
KALI'S ORIGINS AND SYMBOLISM

1. Coburn, *Encountering the Goddess*, 61–62.
2. Nikhilananda, *The Gospel of Ramakrishna*, 271.
3. Magee, *The Yoni Tantra*.
4. Ibid.
5. Ibid.
6. Silburn, *Siva sutra et Vimarsini de Ksemaraja*.

CHAPTER 2.
THE KAULA TRADITION

1. Odier, *Yoga Spandakarika,* 147–64. (Includes the complete text of the *Vijnanabhairava Tantra* in English.)

2. Avalon, *Kularnava Tantra.*

3. Silburn, *Hymnes aux Kali.*

4. Saraswati, *Sri Vijnana Bhairava Tantra.*

6. Sironi, *Vijnanabhairava.*

7. Daniélou, *Le mystère du culte du linga.*

8. Silburn, *Hymnes aux Kali.*

CHAPTER 5.
THE RITUALS OF KALI AND
THE SACRED UNION

1. Fischer-Schreiber, Ehrhard, Friedrichs, and Diener, *The Encyclopedia of Eastern Philosophy and Religion,* 425.

CHAPTER 6.
ADVANCING ON THE KAULA PATH

1. Matsyendranath, *Kaulajnananirnaya Tantra.*

2. Ibid.

3. Ibid.

4. Ibid.

CHAPTER 7.
HYMNS AND SONGS IN PRAISE OF KALI

1. Mookerjee, *Kali, the Feminine Force,* 86–88.

2. Shastri and Ménant, *Hymnes à la Déesse.*

3. Ibid.

4. Ramprasad, *Chants à Kali,* 242

Bibliography

Amazzone, Laura. *Goddess Durga and Sacred Female Power.* Hamilton Books, 2010.

Avalon, Arthur, trans. *Kularnava Tantra.* Delhi: Motilal Banarsidass, 1965.

Coburn, T. B. *Encountering the Goddess: Translation of the Devi-Mahatmya and a Study of Its Interpretation.* New Delhi: Shri Sat Guru Publications, 1992.

Daniélou, Alain. *Le mystère du culte du linga* (The Mystery of the Worship of the Lingam). Paris: Les éditions du Relié, 1993.

Fischer-Schreiber, Ingrid, Franz-Karl Ehrhard, Kurt Friedrichs, and Michael S. Diener. *The Encyclopedia of Eastern Philosophy and Religion.* Boston: Shambhala, 1994.

Grimes, John. *A Concise Dictionary of Indian Philosophy.* Varanasi: Indica Books, 2009.

Lakshmanjoo, Swami. *Kashmir Shaivism: The Secret Supreme.* Edited by John Hughes. Culver City, Calif.: Universal Shaiva Fellowship, 1985, 2003.

———. *Shiva Sutras: The Supreme Awakening.* Edited by John Hughes; Culver City, Calif.: Universal Shaiva Fellowship, 2002.

Magee, Mike. *The Yoni Tantra.* Vol. 2. Harrow, UK: Worldwide Tantra Project, 1995.

Matsyendranath. *Kaulajnananirnaya Tantra*. Translated from Sanskrit [into French] by Dominique Boubouleix. Unpublished.

Monier-Williams, Monier. *Sanskrit-English Dictionary*. 2 vols. Delhi: Motilal Banarsidass, 1990.

Mookerjee, Ajit. *Kali, the Feminine Force*. Rochester, Vt.: Destiny Books, 2014. First published in 1988 by Thames and Hudson.

Muller-Ortega, Paul Eduardo. *Heart of Shiva: Kaula Tantricism of Abhinavagupta in the Non-Dual Shaivism of Kashmir*. Albany: State University of New York Press, 1989.

Nikhilananda, Swami, trans. *The Gospel of Ramakrishna*. New York: Ramakrishna-Vivekananda Center, 1977.

Odier, Daniel. *Tantric Quest: An Encounter with Absolute Love*. Translated from the French by Jody Gladding. Rochester, Vt.: Inner Traditions, 1997.

———. *Das Vijnanabhairava Tantra,* a new translation with commentary. Berlin: J. Kamphausen, Theseus Verlag, forthcoming in 2017 [in German].

———. *Yoga Spandakarika: The Sacred Texts at the Origins of Tantra*. Translated from the French by Clare Frock. Rochester, Vt.: Inner Traditions, 2005.

Ramprasad. *Chants à Kali* (Songs to Kali). Translated from the Bengali by Michèle Lupsa. Paris: Les Belles Lettres, 1982.

Saraswati, Swami Satyananda. *Shree Maa: The Life of the Saint*. Napa, Calif.: Devi Mandir Publications, 1997.

———. *Sri Vijnana Bhairava Tantra: The Ascent*. Munger, Bihar, India: Yoga Publications Trust, 2003.

Shastri, Usha P., and Nicole Ménant, trans. from Sanskrit to French. *Hymnes à la Déesse* (Hymns to the Goddess). Paris: Le Soleil Noir, 1980.

Silburn, Lilian. *Hymnes aux Kali: la roue des énergies divines* (Hymns to the Kalis: The Wheel of Divine Energies). Paris: Institut de civilisation indienne, 1975.

———. *Siva sutra et Vimarsini de Ksemaraja* (Siva Sutra and Vimarsini of Ksemaraja). Paris: Institut de civilisation indienne, 1980.

Singh, Jaideva. *Siva Sutra: The Yoga of Supreme Identity.* Delhi: Motilal Banarsidass, 1979 and reprints.

Sironi, A., trans. from Sanskrit into Italian. *Vijnanabhairava: La conoscenza del tremendo* (Vijnanabhairava: Knowledge of the Great). Milan: Adelphi, 1989.

Wallis, Christopher. *Tantra Illuminated.* Anusara Press, 2012.

Woodroffe, Sir John (Arthur Avalon). *The Garland of Letters.* https://archive.org/details/TheGarlandOfLettersVarnamala2900 (accessed 8/26/15).

Index

About the Author

A teacher of Kashmiri Tantra, Daniel Odier met the tantric tradition through the teachings of the late Kalou Rinpoché in 1968 and remained the Rinpoché's disciple until his passing in 1989. He went to Kashmir to find the source of the tantric tradition and received a mystical initiation from the tantric yogini Lalita Devi. Devi introduced him to the Kaula tradition of Kashmiri Shaivism and initiated him to the Spanda and Prathybijna lineages. He has been her disciple since 1975. His sadhana is described in his book *Tantric Quest: An Encounter with Absolute Love*. In 2004, Odier also received the Ch'an ordination in the Lin t'si and Caodong schools in China as well as permission to teach the Zhao Zhou Ch'an lineage in the West.

Odier has taught literature at the University of California and Eastern religions at the University of Tulsa. He is the author of many books, including *Desire: The Tantric Path to Awakening, Yoga Spandakarika: The Sacred Texts at the Heart of Tantra,* and (under the nom de plume Delacorta) the novel *Diva,* which was made into an internationally acclaimed movie of the same name that has become a cult classic.

Daniel gives workshops transmitting the Kali practices in Europe, Canada, South America, and the United States. He lives in Switzerland.

For more information please visit his website:

www.danielodier.com